In Search of a Better Way

In Search of a Better Way

The Lives and Legacies of
Gary and Matilda Vermeer

Carol Van Klompenburg
Donna Biddle

Published by Vermeer Corporation and the Write Place
Pella, Iowa

ISBN 978-0-9800084-1-8

the Write Place
709 Main Street, Suite 2
Pella, IA 50219
www.thewriteplace.biz

Cover collages and opening portrait of Gary and Matilda Vermeer painted by Tilly Woodward

Book design by Alexis Thomas

Printed by Town Crier Ltd

Manufactured in the United States of America

Contents

Gary and Matilda Vermeer

For 60 years in business,
67 years of marriage,
a lifetime of devotion . . .

Thank you.

Vermeer Corporation

1 Beginnings

There ought to be a better way to do it.

~ Gary Vermeer

Morning Walk

One Sunday morning in 1971, Gary Vermeer slipped on his weathered coat and stepped outside into the January air. It was still early, barely dawn, and he had just enough time for a walk before church.

From his farm two miles east of Pella, Iowa, Gary could see a mile or more in all directions. Across the road to the west, the manufacturing buildings of Vermeer Manufacturing Company stood deserted, as they always were on Sunday. To the north, east, and south, a few scattered farm houses dotted the farmland that stretched for miles toward a flat horizon.

That view was just what Gary liked. Naturally reserved, he didn't like crowds and had little use for the small talk people usually expected. He liked to be busy, and his life, like his conversations, was to-the-point.

Perhaps it was because the depression hit during his impressionable teenage years, perhaps because he was the product of a rural conservative background, or perhaps because it was just his nature—but Gary never was one to waste anything if he could help it—not money, time, or words.

At fifty-two, he was even more sure of himself than he had been as a young man when he had first sold his early inventions to neighbors. A no-nonsense man, he wasn't particularly concerned about trying to make a good impression. He was enjoying success with his business, and he still enjoyed farming. Overall, he was generally satisfied with the life he had built for himself, his wife Matilda, and their three children, now adults and out of the house.

On this particular Sunday morning, Gary didn't walk on his farm but drove north a few miles to a piece of property he owned next to a lake. There, he met his friend and fellow farmer, Arnold Van Zee. Arnold, also in his early fifties, lived near Leighton, about ten miles southeast of Gary. Both early risers, the two men often met for Sunday morning walks.

As a young man, Arnold had gone into the lime quarry business his father had developed. Arnold expanded the business until he owned six rock quarries, crushing as much as a thousand tons a day.[1] But he had tired of it, sold the quarries, and bought calves to raise on the land he owned. Gary had thought that was a good idea: Arnold needed something to do.

So Gary was surprised by Arnold's news that day.

"I'm gonna sell my cows," Arnold said.

"Why in the world you want to do that for?"

"I'm tired of putting up hay."

Years later, Gary recalled that conversation. "I thought if this fella who ought to be in the cattle business is tired of putting up hay, there ought to be a better way to do it."

That conversation would change the lives of thousands and put the Vermeer name into the annals of agricultural history.

Haying Headaches

In 1970, farmers across the nation were binding hay into square bales to feed to their cattle. An improvement over the hot and dusty job of stacking hay, making square bales still required a lot of backbreaking work. And unless a farmer was fortunate to have enough sons or other family members to help, making square bales required farmers to cooperate with neighboring farmers.

Haying was cumbersome and time-consuming. Farmers cut the alfalfa, let it dry at least a day in the field, and raked it into windrows.

A farmer then pulled a square baler behind his tractor. Its hay pickup pulled the alfalfa into the baler where it was packed into a rectangular shape, tied with twine, and pushed up a back-end chute toward a flatbed wagon. Several men with bale hooks took turns grabbing and dragging a bale—each weighed about 80 to 100 pounds—to the back of the wagon where they stacked it.

Baling usually was done three times each summer and required a minimum of three men—more if the farmer had multiple wagon loads. Because rain would ruin the bales, several men needed to immediately unload the wagon into a barn. Whenever a farmer fed a bale to his livestock, he hauled it back from the barn to the feeding trough.

The timing was also tricky. Alfalfa needs to be cut before it flowers purple, then dry in the field before baling. Rain decreases hay's nutrient value, so it is important to work during clear skies. For that reason, farmers often found themselves competing to schedule their hay baling at prime time.

Gary Vermeer wasn't the first to think, "There ought to be a better way to do it." But he was the first to discover a better way.

The day after his conversation with his neighbor, Gary went to see Arnie Mathes in the Vermeer experimental department. Gary liked Arnie's work, and had collaborated with him on past inventions. Gary once told a friend that he valued Arnie because "if he doesn't agree with me, he tells me."

"He had a six-grade education, but he was better than any engineer," Gary said in 1997.

Arnie had been working for Vermeer since 1952. In some ways, he was a lot like Gary. "He could see things in his mind. He was one of the smartest men I know," said Vince Newendorp, an engineer who later came to work with Arnie. "He was very opinionated, but he had enough experience so that in most cases, he was right."

"I think Arnie was a mechanical genius who was also excellent at conceptualizing," said Gary's son, Stan, who later worked with Arnie for a while in the experimental department.[2]

But unlike Gary, Arnie wasn't interested in starting a business. He just wanted to build.

So that Monday morning, Gary and Arnie started building. They started off with two large sheets of plywood and some nails, figuring out a way to build a machine that could make a round one-ton bale—about the size Gary figured that a tractor with a three-prong fork in front could pick up.

They had no idea how big a one-ton bale would be. But they went to work driving nails and trying different options. By late February, they had a prototype. They took it out to an eighty-five-acre field of Gary's to test it.

"We tried and we tried and we tried. And that thing wouldn't turn that bale." Gary recalled.

The problem was that the hay pickup pulled the hay in, turned it once, and then shot it out again before the hay could coil. As Arnie put it, "It would just turn the hay around and puke it out of the front."[3]

So, like dozens of times before and since, Gary improvised.

"I went to the shed, and there were some old fence posts. I took a fence post and I thought, I'll throw it in the baler and see if it will make that thing turn. The fence post was too long, so I sawed it off, and put it in there. You know, when we started that thing, the post turned and the hay went around the post and it baled. I knew we had something."[4]

They had to quit baling when they ran out of fence posts, but as Gary always says when he meets with success, they knew they had something.

They later tried using cardboard tubes about two inches in diameter to replace the fence posts, but adding tubes required the farmer to get off the tractor. They also tried building curved fingers to help coil the hay, and later found that by changing the location of the front roller, these fingers could get the bale rolling.

The first baler formed a bale of hay six feet wide with a seven-foot diameter, and it weighed more than a ton.

Arnie Mathes worked with Gary to develop the first big round hay baler.

Gary knew how much time and effort this new round baler could save. Baling itself shrank from a three-to-five-man chore to a one-man operation. The need to shelter the bales was less urgent because the bales were tight, round, and shed water. The invention made the entire process easier: harvesting, storing, and feeding.

It was revolutionary.

Reaching Farmers

To promote the new machine, Gary relied on what had worked in the past—demonstrations. As he had with other inventions, Gary decided to take his new product to the people who would use it—the farmers—and show them how it worked.

He made arrangements with farmers in ten counties across southern Iowa, where there was a large concentration of cow-calf operations. He put ads in the local papers and posters in coffee shops and sale barns to announce where a week's demonstrations would be. If a farmer missed a demonstration in his county, he could go to the next county and see the baler in operation there.

"I had made a lot of demonstrations with ditchers and stump cutters and all that kind of stuff. You can get ten to fifteen people, and you think you did pretty good. They came out by the hundreds. They had cars backed up by the mile on the road. And people would come in there because, boy, they were ready for something better as far as haying was concerned.

"We made those demonstrations and the next day, you know, you would see a lot of the same people there again. You would say, 'Well, how come you came again?' 'We want to see if it worked two days in a row,' they said. And just in a little bit we had hundreds of orders."[5]

The company asked for a $500 deposit on the machine, the balance to be paid upon delivery. They filled 300 orders that first year, all delivered by May 1972.[6] "At one time, we had 2,000 orders and we ran the whole baler organization with that million dollars," Gary said.[7]

A Pennsylvanian Amish farmer at work with his Vermeer baler in 2006.

They sold the first baler in Guthrie Center, Iowa, for $3,950 plus freight costs. The order was written out longhand on a green order pad.

The first baler, the 706, was discontinued when the smaller 605 series—which made a bale five feet wide with a six-foot diameter—proved to be more practical for farmers.

The baler was the product that launched Vermeer as a truly world-class manufacturer. In just two years—by 1974—Vermeer Manufacturing Company nearly quadrupled in sales.

With what looked like a real success story in the making, the company needed to figure out how it would market and sell the revolutionary round baler.

In one of his weekly management meetings with Harry Vermeer, John Vander Wert, and Carl Boat, Gary suggested finding farmer dealers. Farmers sold seed corn, so why couldn't they sell balers, too?

The company placed ads in newspapers, seeking farmers to sell the balers. Company representatives held coffee times at local coffee shops or Holiday Inns, attracting 20 to 40 potential farmer-dealers each time. Quite often, they turned a customer into a dealer.

They picked regional dealers, then lined up representatives to supervise a state. Wherever hay was sold, they tried to find a dealer. "We found out that hay was raised in places we never dreamed of," said John Vander Wert, a longtime employee. "Farmers got ten percent on the balers they sold. They could do really well on that."

Gary's vision of selling balers through farmer-dealers was a creative move that got the revolutionary new product into the hands of the farmers quickly. The decision also was intended to avoid past experiences when popular Vermeer designs had been taken over by more dominant manufacturers. By putting his products directly into the hands of the farmers, Gary thought the company could circumvent the usual distribution channels and avoid, or at least delay, a similar fate for the baler. Ever since, Vermeer Manufacturing Company has continued the practice, and many of its agricultural dealers are or once were farmers.

In the decades that followed Gary's pivotal distribution decision, Vermeer Manufacturing Company continued to rely on its network of farmer-dealers, who sold the company's newest models of round balers and other agricultural equipment. As farmer-dealers became successful, some transitioned into full-time business people.

In 2008, Vermeer had 450 agricultural distributors in the United States, plus distributors in Canada, Japan, Australia, and New Zealand. In the United States, the agricultural distributors generally fall into one of three categories. The main line distributors are full-time operations that sell and service predominantly Vermeer equipment but may also sell some equipment from other manufacturers. Short-line distributors handle mostly equipment from another manufacturer but have added Vermeer agricultural products into their product mix. Finally, as mentioned before, there still remain the farmer-distributors, farmers who also sell and service Vermeer agricultural products.

Thirteen territory managers, employees of Vermeer Corporation, oversee the agricultural dealers.

Young Tinkerer

Gary was born on September 29, 1918, to Jacob and Anna (Haven) Vermeer. He was born the oldest of four boys on a farm, now part of the Pella Nursery grounds across the road south of Vermeer Corporation. He was a tinkerer from the start, first experimenting in an old summer kitchen behind the house.

Even as a young boy, he knew that if you needed something, you built it. As young boys, he and his younger brother, Elmer (Dutch), built a ladder out of scraps when they wanted to climb and explore. "My dad tore down a barn and built a new one," Gary said. "Boards were lying there so Dutch and I made a ladder from it."

When Gary and Brother Elmer wanted a ladder, they built one.

When Gary finished high school, his dad built a little shop for him in the corner of a chicken house. Though work on the farm didn't allow Gary to spend many summer hours in the shop, he found more time in the winter. He made a stove out of a fifteen-gallon oil drum and burned corn cobs in it. Before Kraft Cheese Company packaged Velveeta in cardboard boxes, the company sold its cheese in long, wooden boxes. Gary used about fifty of these wooden boxes to store his nuts and bolts.

As his brother, John, said years later about the chicken house, "This was the real Plant One. Or maybe it was Minus One."

Gary's tinkering around the farm wasn't unusual. Farmers typically are self-reliant. If something breaks down, farmers work on it until they get it fixed. Fixing things was—and remains today—part of the farmer's lifestyle. But in Gary's case, necessity wasn't the only reason to tinker. He also relished it.

"You would go do chores and probably be done about 9 a.m. and wouldn't start chores [again] until 3 p.m. I spent every day that I could, that I didn't have to do something else, in that shop.[8]

"I started building all kinds of little things. I built a manure loader, and I built a lot of little things, you know, for the neighbors and so forth," Gary said. Another early project was building a cab for his John Deere Model D tractor in 1939.

By the time America entered World War II in December 1941, Gary was 23 years old. He had married Matilda Van Gorp the previous Valentine's Day. His dad had given them a 120-acre farm east of Pella. Matilda's dad had given them some livestock. So Gary and Matilda were ready to begin their lives together as farmers, debt-free.

In those days, long before combines, the Vermeer family had a one-row corn picker. The corn picker, pulled by the tractor, picked the entire ear and moved it by elevator into a nearby wagon.

In 1939, Gary built a cab for his Model D John Deere tractor.

The corn picker certainly beat handpicking, but it really wasn't big enough for the Vermeer farm. Because of wartime rationing, Gary and his younger brother John drove about fifteen miles to the Knoxville county seat to request a permit for a two-row picker from the county rationing board. The board gave them the go-ahead, but only if they would hire themselves out to pick corn for the neighbors, who were strapped for help because so many of the young men were overseas.

"That is what we did. That is what got us into this wagon hoist thing," said Gary. "I had an elevator that I built, so we went around and picked all of our neighbors' corn. I could pull the elevator behind the pickup."

Although they could take their elevator with them, they couldn't drag their overhead hoist—the kind farmers typically used to pick up the entire wagon. Without it, Gary and his dad or brothers had to scoop the ears into the crib—a job hard on back and shoulder muscles.

"I got an idea if we could put those wagons with a hoist under them, then we could take them along, and then we would really have something. Then everybody could use them. So one summer, I built one of those. I intended to put a winch on it with a crank. Before I got to that, I put a pulley on it and took the car and pulled it ahead, and that worked pretty good, so that is the way I left it."[9]

Gary had hooked a cable between the car and the wagon so that when he moved the car forward, the wagon bed tilted up. The wagon itself was stationary; only the wagon bed tilted. Because of gravity, the ears rolled down toward the elevator. Gary created his hoist around 1943.

"You can imagine what a tiring job it was to scoop every load of corn into the elevator at picking time," Gary said. "The hoist was nothing fancy, but it sure beat the scoop shovel."[10]

The wagon hoist helped launch the company.

Gary installed one of his first hoists on a wagon belonging to Albert Engbers, a farmer who lived a half-mile south of Gary. At Albert's farm sale, his brother-in-law Gerrit Vander Wilt bought it, and at Gerrit's farm sale, his son Arvin Vander Wilt bought it. When Arvin, a Vermeer employee, brought the wagon to work one day, Gary noticed it. The two struck a deal that provided Arvin a newer wagon and allowed Gary to acquire the old wagon and hoist. That hoist, still functional, is on display in the Vermeer Museum on the east end of Vermeer Corporation grounds.

History buffs who visit the museum notice the hoist is made of scraps from other old machinery.

"We didn't have much money to buy steel in those days," explained Gary, "so we made do with a lot of scrap. Side rakes were coming in then, and the old dump rakes were no longer used. We would go around and pay farmers a couple of dollars for their old dump rakes and salvage the steel from them.[11]

"The next fall when we went around to buy scrap, everybody said 'Well, build me one of those.' That is the way it started. That is the way the whole Vermeer Manufacturing Company started."[12]

Initially, Gary relied on Van Gorp Welding, a shop in Pella, to help make the hoists. About three years later, demand for his hoists was so strong that Gary decided to start a business and built a 36- by 84-foot cement block building on two acres west of Pella to increase production capacity.

Early Teamwork

Gary started the business with Ralph Vermeer, a second cousin employed at Marion County State Bank. By one account, Ralph had told Gary that if he ever wanted to start a business, Ralph would be interested, and Gary took him up on it. Two other potential investors decided against joining them.

Gary and Ralph signed the articles of incorporation on November 22, 1948, and Vermeer Manufacturing Company was issued the corporate charter by the state of Iowa on January 3, 1949.

Gary built this cement block building in 1948 to manufacture the wagon hoist.

Over the years, Gary has been praised frequently for his ability to find the right person for the job. His decision to go into business with Ralph probably was the first demonstration of this insight.

Unlike Gary, who tended to be brusque, Ralph was smooth and polished. Five years older than Gary, he was outgoing, well-spoken, and a perfect choice for a business partner. While Gary handled engineering and manufacturing, Ralph focused on sales and human relations. As early as 1958, Ralph established an employee profit-sharing plan, a program unusual for its time.

Ralph was also an armchair philosopher. "Everyone we meet in life has some influence on us. Whether it is good or bad depends on how we accept it and approach it," Ralph would say.[13]

Ralph Vermeer

Single for many years, Ralph was a sharp dresser and a ladies' man who enjoyed dating women in the communities where he traveled on business. He loved to step out on the dance floor or play a round of golf.

Ralph also enjoyed a warm relationship with many of the employees. When someone raised the price of a bottle of soda in the company's vending machine, Ralph was upset, said Gloria Van Wyk, a long-term employee. "He went in there and said, 'Who raised that to a dime?' His employees were going to have pop for a nickel."

For several years after incorporation, Ralph continued his job at the bank, while also putting in time to make Vermeer Manufacturing Company a viable business. In the early years, both Gary and Ralph plowed their salaries right back into the company.

Later in life, in 1957, Ralph married Coralyn Phillips Dale, a former beauty queen and a widow with two sons. A diabetic, Ralph was married only five years before he died of a heart attack during a 1962 business trip to Phoenix.

His death was difficult for Vermeer staff, Gloria said. "The employees were devastated because Ralph was, well, they felt Ralph was their big PR person, their HR man."

With Ralph and Gary working together, the company was a family affair from the start. It became even more so when Gary's brother, Harry, joined the company in 1950 and became treasurer in 1954.

Born in 1929, Harry was the youngest of the brothers—eleven years younger than Gary. While Gary saw the mechanical and use possibilities of the equipment and Ralph had relationship and sales sophistication, Harry had an incredible capacity for financial and numerical detail.

Although Gary held the key role in decision-making, he continued to farm—what many have said was his first true passion. Meanwhile, by the mid-1950s, Harry and Ralph worked full-time at the company.

Harry Vermeer

Harry shared Gary's aversion to borrowing. And those who knew him say he could be as demanding as Gary: he worked hard and wanted to make sure he got a full day's work out of employees, too. As head of finance, he was very careful with the fledgling company's money. "To start a new business—especially if you don't want to go into debt—you have to manage every penny," said Steve Van Dusseldorp, Vermeer vice president of finance in 2008.

Once in a while, Harry piloted a plane and flew three employees after work to the Des Moines airport where they had sundaes, recalled Marsha Overbergen, the company's first female employee and first full-time secretary. Mostly, though, Harry was all business. "Harry and I had a desk across from each other. One day Harry explained a way he had come up with saving a lot of money. Ralph said, 'Oh, you have all that Vermeerski blood in you.'"

Harry worked long hours, from 6 a.m. to sometimes 10 p.m. at night. "He had his hand in almost everything," said Arlie Vander Hoek, a longtime employee.[14]

"He handled a lot of the day-to-day problems that came up," said another longtime employee, Keith Nibbelink. Harry took care of the financials, correspondence with the dealers, and was in charge of payroll, production scheduling, and purchasing.[15]

Harry also worked closely with the dealers. "I'd go probably quarterly to dealers and help with their bookwork and taxes," Harry said in a 1998 interview.[16]

"Harry was a mentor to me," said John Vos, who started out demonstrating equipment and later became a Vermeer industrial equipment dealer on the East Coast. "He was a great man and caring about people. Harry was great at administering, the stuff that is not fun for some people. He cared about the details—a banker type, which is what he did after Vermeer."

"He traveled quite a bit, but a lot of times he would be back at night," said Harry's widow, Bernice Vermeer. "Sometimes he flew commercial and was gone for a week. When the kids were small, he missed some of their activities. He always regretted it. But that was just the way it was."

"Saturday was always a day with the kids no matter what," she added. "And Saturday night he would go back to the office after they had gone to sleep."

Harry often went out of his way to be thoughtful. He visited the factory floor regularly to see the employees, and if someone had a birthday, he'd be sure to wish them a happy one. On business letters, he always put a Bible verse at the bottom. "When he died, some people enclosed those letters with the sympathy cards," said Bernice. "That really made me feel good. He planted a seed."

Harry stayed with the company until the mid-1970s when he left and became owner of Marion County State Bank. He was active in the Pella community, and served two terms on its city council. After he had left the company, if Harry saw something nice about a Vermeer employee in the company newsletter or in the town paper, he clipped it and sent it along with a congratulatory note to that person. In his final years, Harry suffered from Parkinson's disease. He died January 19, 2006, following a stroke.

Harry and Gary shared some common traits that led to success. "Harry and Gary were both very mentally sharp. They did not forget much," said John Vos. "And the other trait they shared: they were very fair. You might not always agree with them, but you had to respect what they were doing. People don't get all gooey over Gary, but they have a high respect for him."

Harry's mental gift was for numerical detail, and Gary had the mind of a designer, of an inventor. "Gary had the creative mind. He was the visionary," said John Vos. "Gary was a no-nonsense guy and that sort of takes the politics out of things."

As far as his relationship with employees is concerned, Gary may not have been as personable as Ralph nor as thoughtful as Harry, but employees then, as they have throughout the years, describe Gary as fair.

"Gary treated his workers very well," said Marsha Overbergen. "He was always the same with everyone. He expected them to be good workers, but he treated everyone very fairly. He never had favorites."

Nor was Gary above getting dirty himself.

"When the factory was small, if something needed to be done, he would pick up a piece of steel or go to a drill. He always had his work clothes on," said John Vander Wert.

With Gary's inventiveness, Ralph's salesmanship, and Harry's numerical skills, the company grew fast. In 1949, gross sales were $85,000 with wages totaling less than $9,000. In 1956, sales first reached the $1 million mark.[17]

That kind of growth didn't happen easily or accidentally. Gary had learned he couldn't rest on his laurels—with his very first product.

"I made a little hoist and went out to a lot of dealers around Iowa to see if we could sell them. And we did. But you know, we started manufacturing, and it wasn't very long before it was out of date. John Deere and International came out with hydraulics on their tractors, and so wagon hoists were lifted with hydraulics instead of mechanically. And so that thing didn't do very good, although we did sell a few."[18]

Clearly, if Gary intended to keep manufacturing, the company would need new products. And soon his next major product came along.

Surprising Sales Successes

In the late 1940s, farmers who needed to grind corn or other grains for their cattle often relied on the popular John Deere Hammer Mill. For its time, it was a great help to farmers. But it had one significant problem: the belt would fly off.

Hammer mills were powered by a wide, flat belt linking the hammer mill to a tractor's flywheel. A farmer attached one end of the belt to the flywheel and the other end to the hammer mill. Then he backed up his tractor until there was enough tension on the belt to turn it and run the hammer mill.

The problem, however, was that there was nothing there to keep the belt from flying off. The more corn a farmer fed into the mill, the more stress he put on the belt because it required more horsepower to turn. If the belt was under a lot of stress—especially if it was wet—it would slip and fly off. And if that warm belt flew off into the wet snow. . . ."You could just as well go home because you could not make that belt stay on," Gary said. "And I thought there ought to be some way to do that a little better."[19]

Gary built an angle iron frame and mounted the hammer mill on it. And he used a set of V-belts and pulleys, which were driven by the tractor's power takeoff.

"I could shovel corn in just as fast as I wanted to and it would kill the tractor, instead of the belt flying off. And so, we really knew we had something."

He took it to a farm show in Monticello, Iowa, where a farmer suggested he put it on wheels. Gary thought that was a good idea, added the wheels, and the new Vermeer Pow-R-Drive was ready to market.

To get the word out, Connor Flynn, a Des Moines public relations specialist whose company, Lessing-Flynn, would work with Vermeer Manufacturing Company for years to come, urged Gary to advertise. *Wallaces Farmer*, the most popular farm magazine of the time, was the natural choice. The Iowa-based magazine got its name from the Henry Wallace family. Henry A. Wallace was an Iowa farm boy and editor of the magazine, who left to become Roosevelt's Secretary of Agriculture from 1933 to 1940 and vice president from 1941-1945.

Connor Flynn urged Gary to buy a full-page ad in *Wallaces Farmer* for $1,200. That was too much, Gary told him, probably in just as many words. A half-page ad would cost $600, Con countered. Gary ended up buying a quarter-page ad for $300.

It was all he needed.

Gary remembered his trips to the post office. "They brought those inquiries out with bushel baskets. We had a thousand inquiries in one week, and I had one man working for me. No secretary to answer."[20]

The company ramped up production to make 100 portable power takeoff drives a week for hammer mills and shellers, and did it for years.[21]

"We made 40,000 of those things," Gary told a group of customers in 1997.[22] "And that's when we started making some money. That's the only way you are going to exist in the manufacturing business—by making money. If you didn't know that, you know it now."[23]

The company soon was looking for ways to build on the success of the Vermeer Pow-R-Drive. It wasn't long before that opportunity came along. And, once again, Gary recognized the opportunity because his farming experience told him there had to be a better way.

As a boy, Gary had worked hard with his dad to lay drainage tile as soon as the oats had been harvested. With a team of mules, they plowed a furrow as deep as possible and then used spades to lay the tile.

Tiling was a common practice for farmers because the soil, though rich, tended to be too wet in some places. Tiling improved the drainage. Farmers dug trenches to lay the tile, which at that time were fired clay pipes. During wet weather, the water flowed into the pipes, and was carried through the pipes away from the fields.

Tiling required hard physical labor—just the ingredient to make Gary think that there ought to be a better way.

In 1951, Gary improved on a machine that his neighbor, Leonard Maasdam, had built for trenching. Gary created the Vermeer Model 12 PTO-driven tiling trencher—launching the Vermeer trencher line.

Retired farmers loved trenchers.

"In Iowa, and especially in a lot of midwestern states, there is a lot of tiling going on. And in those days, when the son got old enough to get married and go to the farm, then dad went to town. And dad was so bored in town that he bought one of these ditching machines so he had some work to do," Gary explained. "It was amazing how many farmers—50, 60 years old—came to buy those and to tile their own land and so forth. We sold a bunch of them. And there's where this whole ditching line started from."[24]

Though there were a lot of ditching machines on the market, the Vermeer machine found a niche that proved to be successful. The trencher product line remains a strong seller at Vermeer today.

Blind Alleys

By 1953, after five years of operations, Vermeer Manufacturing Company employed more than 40 people, all under the direction of Gary, Ralph, and Harry.

Working again with Leonard Maasdam, a farmer who also liked to invent, Vermeer introduced the Pow-R-Sprinkler in 1956. It used water velocity to rotate 140-foot sprinkler arms, spreading water in a large circle across the field.

Leonard, together with Gary, Ralph, and Harry, formed Pella Irrigation, a company that distributed Vermeer sprinklers and other irrigation equipment. Vermeer continued to manufacture sprinklers throughout the 1960s and into the 1970s, until sales lagged.

Another product that Vermeer started manufacturing in the mid-1950s was its popular hay conditioner, the Krusher Krimper. It proved to be a successful product for the company, initially.

Gary (seated on tractor) and Ralph test the KrusherKrimper.

As a farmer, Gary knew that an existing hay conditioner already on the market had potential. Crushed hay dries a day quicker than uncrushed hay. Crushing allowed farmers to stack the hay sooner and reduce the chances for rain to ruin the hay as it lay drying in the fields.

But Gary didn't think the current machine worked well enough. So he tinkered, and one Saturday afternoon tried out an improvement on a field across from the Vermeer plant. It worked well.

"In two years' time, we sold 4,000 of those things. And in two years' time we had 29 competitors. The third year, we didn't hardly sell any—we just gave up."[25]

Gary must have been disappointed when Krusher Krimper sales plummeted—just as he must have been disappointed when the introduction of hydraulics made his mechanical wagon hoist obsolete. Farming was always his first love; why didn't he just give up his manufacturing business and go back to full-time farming?

Over the years, he had plenty of opportunities to give up: downturns in the economy and products that simply just failed.

For instance, the Pow-R-Barn Cleaner, which the company produced in 1953, used a conveyor system to remove manure from the barn. It didn't sell well. An end-gate seeder, also produced in 1953, could spread seed over a 30- to 40-foot area behind a wagon. Production ended because there was too much competition.

A grave digger "dug its own grave" shortly after marketing started in 1964, because of lack of interest in the marketplace. A Vermeer street sweeper also debuted around 1964, but it only swept the dirt to one side of the street and couldn't compete with the machines that totally removed the dirt. A circle trencher, built in the 1960s, was a great machine to dig silo foundations. But it was an expensive machine for such a limited use, and the market was quickly saturated.

Over the years there were more failures. What kept Gary going? Why didn't he ever quit?

Just as important, how could the company decide what would or wouldn't work? That was a question friend and longtime Vermeer employee John Vander Wert remembers asking Gary.

"Gary looked right back at me and said, 'If fifty percent of your ideas don't fail, you aren't doing enough.'"

Perhaps that wasn't the first time Gary said those words, but it certainly wasn't the last.

A Fortunate Mistake

Vermeer Manufacturing Company entered the tree stump cutter market in 1957, when Lonnie and Harry Ver Ploeg came to Gary with a prototype machine they thought had promise. Needing to remove stumps from timber land near Pella, the Ver Ploegs had developed a cutter using a twenty-four-inch-wide threshing machine cylinder with cutter teeth.

"They drove over a stump and then drove ahead. And boy, did that ever make a lot of noise," Gary recalled. "But you know, they cut out a stump with that." From that concept, Vermeer Manufacturing Company began developing the first Pow-R-Stump Cutter. The company modified the design, using a drum that made a three-inch wide cut, which company designers believed would work better. However, the drum would have to be pulled through the stump several times to cut the entire stump in three-inch sections.

Alonzo and Harry Ver Ploeg with an early version of their stump removal machine.

"It did work better than a twenty-four-inch, but not a whole lot," Gary recalled.

Sometime later, a fortunate mistake provided just the clue the company needed to develop a truly effective stump cutter.

"The fella who was operating it, I remember he hit the wrong lever, and it went the other way. And that's how we found out the stump cutter cut better one way than it did the other. That thing really took off. We made a lot of those stump cutters."[26]

Making a change in the direction the blade cut through the stump made a huge difference. The machine cut stumps much better when the blade moved sideways across the stump, rather than front to back as initially designed.

The company's introduction of the stump cutter to the market was at an opportune time. Dutch elm disease was sweeping the country, devastating the stately trees that provided shade in so many communities, especially in the eastern parts of the country and the Midwest. The disease first made its appearance in Ohio around 1930, apparently in a shipment of wood from France. It started spreading and by 1970, the disease killed 77 million trees.[27] Vermeer stump cutters were used on many of those stumps.

In the mid-60s, Vermeer introduced another product to its environmental line: the tree spade.

Introduced in the early 1960s, the Vermeer TM-700, a mechanical tree mover, could dig a seven-foot diameter root ball and transplant a tree from one site to another.

Initially, the company introduced the Vermeer TM-700, a mechanical tree moving machine that could dig, transport, and replant large trees economically. By 1967, Vermeer Manufacturing Company produced its first tree spade. The spade was based on Texas nurseryman and inventor Al Korenek's design. The company changed Al's design by converting it into a four-spade version that was smaller and less expensive. This became the TS-44, and more than 400 were sold in its first year. Nurserymen were especially eager for tree spades.

In the 1960s, almost all Vermeer sales were of trenchers, stump cutters, sprinklers, and tree spades. But products were not the only basis for Vermeer Manufacturing Company's success. From the beginning, Gary knew that people were a critical element as well.

*When Gary and Vermeer Manufacturing Company celebrated
their 35th anniversary in 1983, Stan (far right) was president. Bob
and Mary also were involved with the company by that time.*

2 Growing a Company

Approaching people to work was not unusual for Gary. Gary was a master at finding people to do what he wanted done.

~ George Wassenaar, longtime employee

Within a decade, the original Vermeer plant west of town had expanded to include a warehouse, an experimental room, a spray paint booth, and an air-conditioned office. By 1960, Gary, Harry, and Ralph worked there with 140 other employees. And by 1967, the plant had begun to run out of space and built its first building east of town on New Sharon Road.

One key to success in those early days was Gary's ability to pick the right people for the available jobs. And as the company grew, so did the opportunities for the employees.

Advancement Opportunities

Carl Boat

Carl Boat, for example, cleaned floors for Vermeer when he started in 1948. By 1962, as sales manager, he was developing sales and service worldwide, and was nicknamed "Mr. International."[1] In 1976, he became company president.

George Wassenaar says his career at Vermeer was born on a plane trip with Gary.

In the fall of 1960, George was selling cars in Pella and crossed paths with Gary on the west end of town. Gary was ready to fly to St. Louis on a service problem and asked George if he wanted to go along.

"I think that trip might have been the stepping stone that prompted him to ask me to come on board," recalled George. "I think he was just picking my brain. He had the ability to draw conclusions that were pretty accurate within the first hour of conversation. Little did I know a job offer would be following."

The following January, George started a career with Vermeer Manufacturing Company that lasted nearly 30 years. "In everything Gary did, he selected people who could do the job. It was one of the reasons he was so successful," George said.

Another longtime employee, John Vander Wert, recalled a conversation he had with Gary in September 1970, when John was working in the Vermeer accounting department.

"Gary came in the office and said, 'John, I've been fishing quite a bit. I want to do more—I want more time off. I would like you to take care of the experimental room.'

"I said, 'I am an accountant.' He said, 'You were a farm boy. You have mechanical ability.'" John accepted the job.

Another time, Gary thought John could help him find more Vermeer equipment dealers. "I think you have the ability to get along with people and read them pretty good," Gary told John. "Find an area. Put an ad in the Sunday paper. For several days following, go to a motel and interview people. Get it down to two or three, and I will go along and pick the guy we want." John accepted that challenge, too.

Years earlier, Gary had similar conversations with Ed Uitermarkt. Ed started at Vermeer in 1954, earning 95 cents an hour. He worked at the company seven months, quit, then returned later to launch a career that spanned well over 50 years.

At first, Ed made parts in the machine shop. In 1959, Gary asked him to move to the engineering department where he worked on new products. A few years later, Gary again approached him: "I would like you to take over the engineering department."

Ed hesitated. He knew Gary was demanding. "I don't know. I might make a lot of mistakes."

"I make mistakes, too," Gary said. "If you make mistakes, you just have to go fix them."

Ed remembers well one mistake he made close to Gary. Too close.

"Over at old Plant 1, we had made a drop hammer and we were experimenting outside of the plant. Gary was standing there, and it blew a hose and sprayed him with oil, just drenched him. It was lucky the oil wasn't hot; it was just warm. He didn't say too much. He just kind of laughed it off."

Gary was especially interested in employees with proven initiative. Some said that he figured the best employees were farmers with dairy cows because they could be counted on to work hard and be on time.

One thing was clear: a good education didn't give a job candidate any advantage with Gary, particularly engineers.

"You can't educate imagination. You either have imagination or you don't have," Gary said.

In June 1977, Vince Newendorp became one of the first degreed engineers at Vermeer. "When I became a manager, Gary told me, 'I want you here at 6:30 so we can walk through the projects, and I'll be back at 12:30.' That was the schedule we kept."

It was a strict schedule, but not inflexible. "Gary has always been fair," said Vince. "If something came up, he understood that."

Mentoring Moments

Gary could be flexible, but he was not an easygoing boss.

"One day, I'm in my office," Vince remembered, "and all of a sudden coming up the stairs, I hear boom, boom, boom, boom. And through my door is Gary

Gary often popped into managers' offices unannounced. Here, Gary is in his own office in October 1973.

Vermeer. His first words were, 'Vince, what kind of a department are you running right now?'"

Vince had no idea what Gary was talking about. He soon learned. A couple of prankster engineers had superglued someone's steel-toed shoes to the top of his toolbox. A technician was trying to pry them loose with a screwdriver when Gary walked in.

"You figure out what you're going to do, and I'll come back," Gary told Vince. So Vince investigated and took appropriate disciplinary action. "Gary came back and said, 'Well, what did you do?' I told him. He got this grin on his face and walked out."

Today, Vince sees Gary's response to that incident as Gary's way of mentoring him. "It shows integrity. He trusts people to run an area of the company." Vince also sees it as a demonstration of Gary's values. "When you're on the clock, he expects a full day's work."

Popping in to managers' offices unannounced was common, motivating many managers to pay attention to details.

For instance, from his finance officers, Gary always wanted to know four things:
1. The amount of cash in the bank
2. The amount of inventory in the yard
3. The amount that dealers owed the company
4. The profit margin

On any given day, Gary could appear at the door of the Vermeer finance officer demanding to know those figures—although normally, those numbers are calculated once a month. "I soon learned to always know where we were cash-wise," said Steve Van Dusseldorp, Vermeer vice president of finance.

When Gary started popping in to his office, Steve wasn't entirely sure if those figures were something Gary really wanted to know, or if it was his way of ensuring his new employee stayed on top of finances. "Without having had a college course on how to be a mentor, he had a built-in sense of how to teach people," said Steve. "There were certain things he learned through experience, and he wanted other people to know. He wasn't going to schedule a meeting, but he would take advantage of the opportunities that arose."

Similarly, Al Van Dyke, retired territory manager for agricultural sales, said Gary often asked him about inventory when he was a sales manager. Al quickly learned to have those numbers in his head—always. "You'd better have the right numbers, because he'd know it right away if you didn't. He knew the answers before he asked."

Gary mentored his offspring, too.

Steve Van Dusseldorp remembers being part of a meeting—perhaps in the early 1990s—with Gary and his two children who now lead the company, Bob Vermeer and Mary Andringa. A senior manager was making a proposal for a capital improvement. The manager presented a logical and reasonable case.

"I don't think we want to do that right now," Gary told him. As soon as the manager left, Gary turned to Bob and Mary. "That's probably a good idea, but you can't say yes to every good idea." Gary again used a situation to impart a lesson. A company may have many people with good ideas, but a company can't afford to stretch itself too thin.

Other times, Gary was more explicit about the company's financial situation, and shared his formula for a healthy company: no more than 20 percent of sales in inventory, 10 percent in receivables, and 10 percent in fixed assets.

"Profit and cash were more important to Gary than growth," said Bob Vermeer. "Growth was fine, but not the key thing. Right after cash, he wanted to know: do we have too much inventory? He could see the number of units sitting around. He didn't like to see a lot of iron back there."

Gary especially never wanted to see his company in debt. "If you don't have any debt you don't go broke," Gary said in 2007. "If we had to borrow money for a project, we didn't do it. We borrowed very little."

"He'd say that the farmers in debt during the Depression couldn't make it, but the farmers who weren't in debt could make it," recalled Steve Van Dusseldorp. "Many, many times he talked about the Depression. He was always concerned about the company's ability to weather a downturn."

"Gary laid the ground work for the company; he had strong principles," added John Vos, a Vermeer dealer. "No debt was a strong principle, and it was unusual. Today, I have no debt. I got those principles from dealing with Vermeer. You want to be financially sound. And to be financially sound, you have to deal from a position of strength. Gary dealt from a position of strength—and what he built is going into the third generation. He must be so proud of that."

Flying Service

Shortly after the company's launch, Gary started doing business with Lindsay Brothers, a farm distributor based in Minneapolis with a branch office in Des Moines.

Gary wanted to visit people in Kansas and Missouri, and asked the distributor to fly him both places in one day.

"He liked to fly, and was glad to fly for us. I thought that was a great way to go because with a car it would take a couple of days," recalled Gary. Gary had flown in a small airplane before, but he was really impressed he could see a couple of distributors in one day and be home at night.

"Generally it was important to me to be home at night, but I also stayed away sometimes," he said. "So I started taking flying lessons. Right here in Pella. I took lessons on a Piper Cub. You need a certain amount of hours and pass a flying test. I didn't have any problem with that." Gary obtained his first license in February of 1950.

After the 1971 introduction of the round baler, Gary often flew employees to meet customers and service their equipment, sometimes sharing Matilda's egg sandwiches. They flew in Gary's Bonanza, or, if they needed to land in a small place, they flew in Gary's Super Cub. Made by Piper, this small yellow plane carried only two people in tandem—one behind the other. It was a slow plane with maximum cruising speeds of 165 to 185 kilometers per hour, but it could land in a hayfield.

"Many of us learned to fly on that Super Cub," recalled George Wassenaar. "It was a little plane with a super engine, and was capable of very short field takeoffs. If a farmer was having trouble in a hayfield, we could actually land on a good level hayfield. Gary did that many times."

Gary and Harry had licenses, of course, as did Ralph before his death in 1962. But many others obtained licenses, too.

"Gary wanted all his staff to fly," said George. "John [Vander Wert] had a license. Carl [Boat] had a license. A lot of guys had licenses. It made us pretty tough competitors."

George Wassenaar

George has never forgotten the first time he flew with Gary, that time he accompanied Gary on a service call to St. Louis in the Bonanza just before Gary hired him.

After they'd been in the air awhile, Gary put the plane on autopilot, leaned back, and closed his eyes. "You watch for other aircraft," Gary told George. "I'm going to take a nap." It was George's first time in a small airplane.

Ed Uitermarkt had a similar experience when Gary needed a nap on the way to Indianapolis. "I'll set it at 10,000 feet. Watch the altimeter, and watch for planes," Gary told Ed.

"I didn't know a thing about planes," Ed recalled.

Going International

To make a business successful, Gary has said, you first need a product and secondly, you have to be able to sell it. Production comes third because you don't need to produce anything unless you can sell it.

Although Gary was a farmer and tinkerer at heart, he never underestimated the importance of sales.

"He was a natural marketer. Lots of people are inventive, but Gary also knew how to make something work, market it, and run a business. That makes him unique—part of a special subset of people. That is what founders are made of," said son-in-law Dale Andringa.

While Vermeer agricultural products are mostly sold through a network of agricultural equipment distributors, most of them farmers, the industrial products are marketed and sold differently.

In the late 1950s, with the trencher and the stump cutter both selling well, the company decided to establish Vermeer-exclusive dealerships—the forerunner of today's industrial dealerships. The first such dealership was opened in Findlay, Ohio, in 1960 by Art Van Weelden, who had been the first salesman at Vermeer.[2]

The second dealership was in Iowa. Initially called Pella Irrigation and Equipment, it sold a variety of Vermeer products, including irrigation equipment. Stockholders included Gary and Harry Vermeer, Leonard Maasdam, Carl Boat, and Case Vander Hart. Additional Vermeer-exclusive dealerships soon followed.

Even before Vermeer set up Vermeer industrial dealerships domestically, the company was selling product internationally. Beginning in the early 1950s, the fledgling company sold abroad through export managers in New York City. By 1955, Vermeer machines were in use in Europe, Asia, and Latin America. Ralph Vermeer is credited for much of the company's early worldwide sales, and those efforts laid the foundation for the company's subsequent international success.

Harry Vermeer speaks during an October 1962 sales meeting. Gary is sitting on Harry's right.

During the 1950s, personnel from Vermeer Manufacturing Company worked with Jan de Bas to start Vermeer Holland, which was incorporated in the Netherlands to handle sales, and later, some manufacturing in Europe. As the years progressed, Vermeer Holland started manufacturing more products, and in 1979, Vermeer Holland became a separate and independent entity owned by Jan De Bas that manufactured some of its own products but sold some of Vermeer Manufacturing Company's products as well. At the same time, Vermeer Manufacturing Company created Vermeer International, a wholly owned subsidiary in Goes, the Netherlands, to focus solely on international industrial product sales. Jaques de Jonge was its first managing director.

In 2008, the international sales group is made up of three groups. The Pella group handles Latin America. The Vermeer regional office in Goes, the Netherlands, covers Europe, the Middle East, and Africa. The regional office in Singapore covers Asia and Australia.

Currently, Vermeer Corporation offers sales, parts, and service through a worldwide industrial dealer network consisting of 115 North American industrial dealers and 63 international dealer locations, in addition to its more than 400 agricultural distributors. Vermeer has a global focus as it has industrial dealerships located in 51 countries and every continent except Antarctica.

Another reason for Vermeer sales success has been the company's early recognition of the need to train dealers and their service technicians. In early years, Harry Vermeer had traveled to the dealers and helped them with bookkeeping and taxes. The company began its first service schools in the mid 1960s—an important tool enabling dealers and their service technicians to provide excellent service to Vermeer customers.[3]

That training continues. More than 100 service technicians and more than 100 parts and service managers annually attend factory schools at Vermeer headquarters. In addition, the company provides web conference training, regional service training, and additional sales force training.

"Vermeer has been good to dealers," said Dealer John Vos. "Dealers have a relationship with Vermeer Corporation that no one else in the industry has. We are a team. A husband and wife don't always agree, but they have respect for each other and work through their differences. That is the way it is with Vermeer Corporation and the dealers."

Founded on Principles

Biblical principles are at the heart of the company's philosophy.

Gary's moral compass is evident in what the company calls its 4P Philosophy. As a man of few words, Gary never articulated the philosophy—that just wasn't his way—but from the beginning he operated the company in a way that demonstrated the importance he placed on the four Ps: Principles, People, Product, and Profit. It fell to the second generation—Mary Andringa, Bob Vermeer, and his wife Lois—to specifically articulate the philosophy. In its sixtieth year, the company functions by that philosophy as much as ever.

The 4P Philosophy is illustrated by a wheel. The Biblical principles that form the center hub of the wheel indicate the company is to be guided by principles such as striving for excellence, stewardship of resources, and honoring the Golden Rule: "Do for others what you want them to do for you."

Circling around the hub of Principles are the other three Ps:

People: Vermeer values its employees by providing a stable work environment, opportunities for growth within the company, professional development and company profit sharing.

Product: Vermeer provides customers with valuable products and business solutions, helping gain and retain customers' respect and loyalty.

Profit: Vermeer seeks to attain a profit that will finance company growth and finance the needed resources to gain a competitive advantage within the industry.

Over the years, Gary demonstrated his reliance on this philosophy. Already in the 1950s, he hired disabled workers and later hired refugees when other companies were reluctant to do so. As early as 1950, Gary and Ralph developed a policy that the company would give a portion of profits to charity, and by 1958 they had established the Vermeer Foundation. Later, the company developed still other ways to help, such as providing equipment and volunteers to help clean up after natural disasters.

Gary's principles held fast even when tested.

"When we were a small company, farmers would drive in on Sunday thinking they would pick up parts. Vermeer Manufacturing Company would not open up the business to sell them parts. But they could call us Monday morning, and we would fly the parts out to them," recalled Marv Vander Werff, who started his association with Vermeer in 1954.

"It would have been so simple to call someone and say, 'Run out and get this guy what he needs.' I always thought that was a pretty neat thing—that they practiced what they preached."

Gary also encouraged employees toward Sunday rest. "The Vermeers were very religious. When we used to travel, they would recommend—but they didn't say we had to—that if I was in Dallas, Texas, on Saturday night, they would prefer that I was still in Dallas, Texas, on Monday morning," said Marv. "Ralph was the same way. I remember once in Gallup, New Mexico, instead of flying home we stayed over and went to church."

When threatened by labor unrest, Gary chose to do what he could to work with his employees. Being fair was important to him.

Around 1969, there was some uneasiness in the plant. The word was that a Vermeer employee had a friend or relative who worked for Parsons Manufacturing 30 miles to the northwest, in Newton. That company also made trenchers, and they were a union shop.

Some Vermeer employees thought maybe they weren't getting a fair shake and held a couple meetings off the premises.

"Gary didn't like it because he figured we were treating the people fairly," recalled John Vander Wert.

So Gary decided to organize a committee of employees to meet with management. "We would meet with them as management and lay out some ground rules and tell them we wanted to hear their problems," said John. "You talk with the people you work with."

They also decided to visit six comparable plants in Iowa—three chosen by employees, three by management. After visiting these companies and making their comparisons, management promised to pay average or above-average wages. Vermeer made a few adjustments, and employee unrest subsided.

Celebrations and Rewards

Perhaps the company's most popular tradition is to distribute year-end bonuses, based on the year's profit—a policy established as early as 1958, apparently at Ralph's behest.

Vermeer Corporation still holds an annual year-end meeting with all employees to discuss business successes and upcoming goals, as well as to announce year-end bonuses awarded to employees based historically on the company's profitability and an employee's longevity—as much as nearly 15 percent of their base pay. The bonuses aren't guaranteed—and there have been years when poor sales prevented the company from paying them. But in good years—and most years have been good for the company—employees typically receive the bonuses near year's end, finding it useful to fund Christmas gifts, pay off debts, or add to retirement savings.

Vermeer employees gather in the Global Pavilion for the year-end meetings. This one was in 2006.

Two of Gary's children, Co-Chief Executive Officers Bob Vermeer and Mary Vermeer Andringa, host the multi-media meeting held in the Vermeer Global Pavilion's arena, a cavernous space in a 75,000 square-foot building built on the factory campus in 1997. These meetings are a mix of the serious and the upbeat. They convey appreciation for employees' hard work during the past year and motivate them for the following one.

In the 1950s and 1960s, the annual meetings under Gary's tutelage were no less a production, though of a different sort. In the early years, the Christmas parties, as they were known then, were held at the Pella Country Club. One of Bob Vermeer's earliest memories of these is when a magician hired to entertain the employees sawed secretary Marsha Overbergen in half.

By the 1960s, the meetings had grown larger and were held in the Pella Christian High School gym. Spouses and children were invited to these dinner meetings—much anticipated dress-up events. One longtime employee recalls sewing special matching dresses for her children.

Some years they played a mock version of a show popular on radio in the 1940s and later on TV: "Doctor I.Q.: The Mental Banker." On that show, the host asked audience members questions. If they answered correctly, they won a few silver dollars. The Vermeers also handed out silver dollars for a correct answer.

Young and inexperienced, Gloria Van Wyk did her best to avoid being picked to answer a question. "I didn't want to be picked out. I remember looking away and trying to be discreet." But of course, in 1958 she was singled out. Her question: Who is the new pope? Gloria was happy to answer correctly: Pope John XXIII.

Another time, unbeknownst to the employees, the company brought in a comedian from Kansas City. Employees thought he was a nuclear rocket scientist hired to give a speech after the meal.

During the meal, the man acted nervous, spilled his water glass, and wiped his brow with his shirt sleeve. "Then he got up to speak, and he was so nervous, he took his tie and wiped his forehead with his tie. He'd start a sentence out, and his thought would transfer to another thought in the middle of the sentence," said Keith Nibbelink, a longtime employee. "Nobody dared to laugh. We were so embarrassed because we thought this wasn't good at all."

Eventually, one person snickered, then several. Belly laughs soon followed as the joke on the employees became apparent.

In 1964, when the year-end event became too big for the school, Vermeer moved it to The Dutch Buffet, which included a restaurant, roller skating rink and bowling alley that Gary had a hand in developing. Afterwards, the employees went roller skating. Gary joined in. "Gary loved to have fun. He loved to bring employees along to have fun," said Gloria.

Canada Outings

Probably the biggest—most generous—way that Gary brought employees along for fun was when he took employees fishing in Canada.

Gary piloted the plane that left Pella at 7 a.m. on a Monday morning. By early afternoon, he and his guests were fishing on a Canadian lake. On these trips, he often piloted a Bonanza, a plane first introduced by Beechcraft in 1947 that became a classic with its distinctive V-shaped or "butterfly" tail. It carried three people plus a pilot.

Employees say Gary was different on these trips than he was in the office. Away from the office, he wanted to have fun and forget about business. He became less serious, less demanding.

"On fishing trips, he still called all the shots, but he was different," said Larry Groenenboom, a friend and long-term employee. "He cleaned all the fish. It was a good experience because I will never go to Canada again in the way that I did with him. He would go to virgin lakes that no one else went to. And there were always lots of fish."

"I'm not a fisherman," said Steve Van Dusseldorp, who has been fishing only a half-dozen times since he fished with Gary in 1988. "To go fishing in Canada is a whole different experience. His fishing was like no other fishing I've had in Iowa. The number of fish you caught was dependent on how fast you could bait your hook."

John Vander Wert recalled a fishing trip he took with Gary and Marv Ver Heul, now retired from Vermeer. Marv was in the shower house, which had a lock on the outside, probably to keep it from banging in the wind. "We locked the door, and he couldn't get out," said John. "He was yelling and hollering. Gary laughed so hard he had to take his glasses off and wipe his eyes."

When Vermeer Manufacturing Company turned forty in 1988, Gary decided to treat forty employees to a week-long fishing trip in Canada. The company held contests to pick some of them, and awarded the trip to others based on their accomplishments. Gary rented the entire campground for the employees, and every day he took as many as possible on his floatplane to a remote fishing site while the others fished around the campground.

"My trip to the lake on the floatplane was short because the weather was bad. Gary had to fly too low. He was concerned about losing his bearings," recalled Steve Van Dusseldorp, one of the employees chosen for that trip. At first, Steve only noticed that the clouds were low and also that Gary wasn't talkative. That puzzled him, because he had heard that Gary talked a lot while flying, pointing out wildlife and other sites of interest. When Gary finally landed the floatplane at their home base, he turned to the others on the plane: "That's about the worst I've ever flown in."

Steve, for one, was glad Gary hadn't said anything until they landed. He thinks Gary wouldn't normally have flown in those conditions. "I think he felt pressured to get everybody out to the remote lake."

Gloria Van Wyk, too, was one of the trip winners that year, though she believes she was mostly chosen to be a roommate for Romona DenBesten, a Vermeer dealer from the East Coast who had won.

The two women flew to Canada a day before the others. "We enjoyed Gary and Matilda by ourselves. I saw a whole new side of them," Gloria recalled. "They took us to an outpost, and they prepared our meal in the wilderness. It was an awesome treat to be able to do that."

The Vermeers took them by floatplane and by inflatable boat to their fishing site, where the couple worked as they have done so many times through the years—like clockwork. "It was total teamwork. Each of them knew what they needed to do," said Gloria.

Romona caught the biggest fish that week. "Today my fish continues to hang behind my desk in Castleton and to this day still receives its share of attention," she wrote in a memoir to Gary in 1988.

"I looked at that as a special time," said Gloria. "Not too many employees got to do that."

The number of invited employees increased over time. Almost every year, Gary took some fishing. The company selected a number of people who had been promoted that year as well as some monthly winners of Expect the Best—Vermeer Corporation's version of an employee-of-the-month recognition.

In 1982, the year Kevin Arkema was promoted from welder to foreman, he got a call at home informing him that he had won the trip. Instantly, Kevin knew he was one of a lucky few. "That was a very highly prized reward, to go fishing with Gary."

Along with two other employees, Kevin boarded a Vermeer plane on the runway behind the plant and flew to International Falls, Minnesota, where they went through customs. From there, they flew to Perrault Falls, Ontario, where they met Gary and Matilda. Matilda flew back to Iowa on the Vermeer plane, while Kevin and the two other employees joined Gary in his pickup for a ride to the campground.

A half hour after arriving at the camp, they were fishing. "Gary had the whole day planned," said Kevin. "And every day was a different lake."

Using his floatplane, Gary flew the men to a new lake each day, where he had built a dock to tie up the plane. On the way, Gary swooped down to give the men a closer look at the wildlife. Because air currents vary over water and land, the ride can be a bit bumpy, and it set Kevin's stomach to churning.

"All of a sudden, Gary calls 'MOOSE!' and dive bombs. I had to open my lunch box because I lost my dinner that day."

Gary carried a portable outboard motor in the plane, which he put onto a rowboat that he had stashed in the brush next to the lake. At noon, Gary got a stove out of a box, also hidden in the brush, and he fried fish. The men sat on nearby flat rocks to eat. After lunch, they cleaned up and stashed the stove away. They fished all day and returned to the cabin for dinner. Just forty steps from the water, the cabin was comfortable, carpeted, nicely furnished. And definitely clean—Matilda's doing, Kevin thought.

They opened the refrigerator and cooked what they saw—often burgers or steaks. At least once, they made a salad using fixings Matilda had provided.

Before the trip, Gary had brought farm equipment into Kevin's plant for repair, but Kevin hadn't had much contact with the company founder. Even so, Kevin found talking with him easy. "It was like you were at home," Kevin recalled. "The conversation was very comfortable—it was like being with your grandpa."

After supper, the men listened to the radio. Often, they sat in lawn chairs in the front of the cabin, talking, listening to the loons, and watching the sun set.

Another employee, Harold N. Meinders, won't forget a trip he won in 1973. A storm in the middle of Minnesota forced Gary to land. Harold remembered:

> We couldn't just sit idly by and wait. Gary called back to the factory and asked for the baler dealer closest to where we were. Then he called the dealer and he came and picked us up. We went to his place and were loaned a vehicle to go out to a farmer who had purchased one of the new Vermeer big round balers. We found him in the field trying to bale long grass hay where the stubble was quite tall. He was having trouble getting the baler to work. When he stopped, he said, "I would certainly love to talk to the guy who designed this machine." Gary said, "You're talking to him." The man went on to tell Gary his frustrations. Gary called the factory again, and the next day Arnie Mathes went up to see the problems. Gary and our group continued on our fishing trip and had a very enjoyable time."[4]

Without exception, Steve, Gloria, Harold, Kevin, and all the others who were fortunate enough to share a Canadian fishing trip with Gary said it was something they would never forget.

"Gary enjoyed fishing and because of him there were a lot of employees throughout the plant who had an opportunity to fish. He took the people doing the jobs for him. They were the people who were important in the organization," said George Wassenaar. "That was something union guys never had."

Always Gary's Workshop

Gary had started his business because he needed a wagon hoist for his farm work. Subsequently, he made the power takeoff drive for the hammer mill because he was tired of the drive belt flying off his own hammer mill. He started inventing to make his life and the lives of his neighbors easier.

It was only natural that when he needed mechanical work done, he continued to return to his workshop—even after it had grown from the corner of a chicken coop to a 1.5 million-square-foot manufacturing facility.

His employees testify he usually wanted the work done sooner rather than later.

"In 1973, Gary was planting corn," recalled Ed Uitermarkt. "I don't know if the piece was on the planter or the disc, but he needed some welding and fixing done on it. It was 7 a.m., and I had just started work."

"How soon can you have it done?" Gary wanted to know.

"By noon, easy," Ed told him.

As always, Gary wasn't ready to be patient. "I need it quick. Put the whole department on it, and I'll be back in two hours to pick it up."

"We did, and it was done in two hours," Ed recalled.

Vince Newendorp, head of the experimental room in the early 1980s, recalls when Gary walked into the room with another project request. Gary had bought land across the Skunk River from property he already owned, and he wanted a walking bridge across the river. The two discussed the design, and Vince told him preliminary designs could be done by the end of the week. "No," Gary told him. "I'd like the bridge done by the end of the week."[5]

Gary's timeline was typical. "In the experimental department, we knew our first job was for Gary. If he needed something for the farm, you dropped what you

The walking bridge over the Skunk River

were working on and you did it," said Vince.

Kevin Arkema recalls a time when he was working as a welder in Plant 3, Gary wanted an extension on his combine axle so that he could put on float tires, allowing him to drive over wet ground more easily. "He could have gone to John Deere for a couple hundred dollars, but no, he wanted it made. Then he liked it so much, he wanted another."

Even in his later years, Gary had a tinkering spirit and made use of the expertise at his factory just across the road from his home and farm.

In Gary's mid-80s, when walking became more difficult, he bought a scooter to get around. While making the purchase, he and Matilda also looked at a car carrier for it.

"Let's go," he abruptly told Matilda.

"Well, aren't we going to get this?" she asked.

"We can easily make one," Gary told her.

"That is part of the fun for him. Besides, he didn't want to spend all that money," said daughter-in-law Lois Vermeer.

Soon after, Gary went into the plant to talk with Larry Groenenboom about building a car carrier for the scooter. Gary wanted it lightweight and strong. They built a model, but it dragged on Gary's driveway. So Larry made some changes. "Gary wanted the edges six inches tall, so the cart wouldn't roll off. He didn't want to chain it down," Larry recalled. That meant that Larry needed to make a ramp, which required plywood—a scarce item in an equipment manufacturing facility.

"I showed him what we had, and he chose three-quarter-inch finished oak plywood. That's expensive stuff, maybe $50 a sheet. But that didn't bother Gary."

They put hinges on it, and it worked great. Altogether, Larry worked on it about a day and a half. It probably cost more than the ready-made one.

"He was pretty proud of it. We still store it in the shop, and we put it on the car for him when he wants it."

A Man of Paradox

Gary's generosity—personally and through the company and foundation—has been huge. Magnanimous probably doesn't cover it. But his abrupt no-nonsense manner can sometimes be off-putting. Gary says what he means, he seldom engages in a conversation if the topic doesn't interest him, and he doesn't generally bother to soften his words with tact.

"In the early days, there could be confrontations between the dealers and Gary. He wasn't diplomatic. So there was sometimes conflict, controversy, and arguing. My approach was: you tell me the game and the rules, and I will figure out how to play it," said John Vos, who started as a factory demonstrator right out of high school and eventually become one of the company's largest dealers.

Gary at a July 1982 meeting with industrial dealers

"He was stubborn, but he was generous. He was demanding, but he was rewarding," said Arlie Vander Hoek, a 38-year employee who started out at Vermeer with cleanup duties and later came to oversee operations of all the plants.

"Gary was a fairly intimidating man. He was like EF Hutton: when he spoke, people listened," said Vince Newendorp, who started as an engineer and later headed the company's Administration group. "When he said the sky was red, I said, 'Yes, the sky is red,' and I told everyone else the sky was red."

"There were times I didn't agree with him, but I didn't tell him that," said another long-term employee, Keith Nibbelink. "If there was something you knew wasn't going to work, it was better to go ahead and make it, and then show it to him."

Yet Gary is well-respected. "Gary is one of the men I really respect. He has given me a lot of opportunities," Vince said.

Few bosses are as serious about work as Gary. He demanded a full day's work. In the early days, he didn't even want people to waste time drinking coffee at their desks. "Gary didn't like two guys in a pickup either, because somebody was doing something and somebody was doing nothing," said Arlie Vander Hoek. To ensure he got a full-day's work, Gary was known at day's end to have counted the bricks that part-time construction help had laid.

The no-nonsense attitude that kept Gary's conversations abrupt and his employees on task also compelled him to make the big decisions.

"In meetings, Gary was always fair. He was always firm in his convictions," said John Vos. "At big meetings you would be discussing something for a while. Gary would stand up and say, 'This is the way it is.' And the conversation stopped right there. Not that he was wrong. He was in charge, and you knew he was in charge."

Marv Winick, a retired corporate attorney whose firm often represented the company and the family, also became accustomed to his client's abrupt decision-making. Marv and fellow staff members lived and worked in the Des Moines area, about an hour's drive away from the factory, so they rose rather early one morning for a 7 a.m. meeting with Gary in Pella.

Marv remembered, "We were there about ten minutes, and Gary said, 'That's fine,' and walked out. And that was the end of the meeting. That was Gary. He was very brief—and quick to make a decision."

Gary could be quite adamant about his opinions, Marv added. "The funniest incident was when I was doing a will for Gary. It was probably forty-some pages long. He looked at it and said he was not going to sign it."

"It's too long," Gary said.

Marv explained that Gary's will was fairly complicated and needed to be that long. But Gary was adamant. He had seen plenty of old abstracts in his time that contained wills, and none were that long.

"If you can't get that down to fewer pages, I'm going to go to another lawyer," Gary told Marv.

"So I went back and cut out what I thought could be cut out, and I put it on longer paper and in smaller type, and got it down to ten pages, and he signed it."

Marv recalled that wasn't the only time Gary humbled him. "He'd say, 'I haven't always listened to you, and I have done alright.'"

Quite likely it is because of Gary's reputation for seriousness at work that a particular snowball story has become a legend around the plant. Dealer Art Swank, a principal player in the story, tells about a time when he was working at the factory:

> Early in my employment with Vermeer, Roger Van Noorden and I were outside the factory on a winter day on break when we decided that the next person that exited the door was going to get snowballed. Each of us was ready with several snowballs ready to go when the door opened. Not seeing who it was, we let go. The door shut, then opened again. We reloaded and started again, and that's when we heard Gary's voice from behind the door telling us it might be a good idea to stop.
>
> This story has been told so many times by so many people, I have finally decided to set the record straight.
>
> Gary didn't even get hit.

Gary didn't have much patience for shenanigans at work. If he didn't like something that was going on, he didn't mince words.

After Vermeer opened its new plant east of Pella, the company organized an open house for the public. As part of the festivities, the company planned to parade equipment inside the new plant to show the public. John Vos intended to demonstrate a Vermeer T-600 Track Trencher.

"Most guys just drove by the crowd. I came out at full speed (perhaps five miles per hour), and instead of turning 90 degrees left, I accomplished the same thing by turning 270 degrees right. I had to practice for that because when you stop turning, the equipment is still going to keep sliding." John certainly didn't want to hit another piece of equipment or one of the poles supporting the new building. "Gary saw me practicing, and he told Carl Boat: 'If he wipes out one of those poles, you fire him.'

"If you wanted to go out and have a fun time, Gary wasn't the guy to go out with," added John. "He was serious. But remember, I was nineteen, and he was older. He was more serious-minded."

Although he enjoyed telling jokes at the company Christmas parties, very, *very* few people have seen Gary joke around at the office. Keith Nibbelink, who started at Vermeer in 1954, is one of the lucky ones.

It was in one of the early years at Vermeer that Gary showed up at the plant carrying a cage. The cage was completely closed off on one end, but had a tail sticking out. It was a ferret's tail, Gary told those who gathered around. It was a mean animal, he said, so mean that it had bitten someone's finger off the week before.

"Gary went on and on with his story, and by that time, everyone was hanging over the cage trying to see it," Keith recalled. The cage had a door that was spring-loaded, and Gary knew just the right moment in his story to hit that spring. "The lid flew open, and that tail flew out into the group of people," Keith recalled. People ran, and fast. "The first time, I ran, too, but then it was so much fun watching the reaction of people. They would just take off and scatter.

"A lot of times, Gary would be a sober, strict person, but he had his different side to him, and sometimes he enjoyed a good joke."

Outside of work, Gary relaxed a bit more. During these times, he was more likely to instigate a bit of fun, no matter what time of day.

Early in 1985, Vince Newendorp and his new wife, Monica, had been back from their honeymoon only a week or two when they were abruptly awakened from a sound sleep.

"At 5 a.m., the doorbell is ringing. People are pounding on our door. It scared us half to death," Vince said. He quickly scurried to the front door. "And there at the door was Gary Vermeer and there were twenty people behind him. He walked in and everyone followed."

It turned out to be Gary's way of shivareeing the new couple. Everyone brought pots and pans, a toaster, eggs, bread, and all the other necessary ingredients for an early-morning shivaree. "Gary was at the stove cooking and directing traffic. We had breakfast, and Gary was having a hey-ho time.

"Within an hour, they were gone. Gary said, 'See you at 6:30.' The switch was flipped, and it was all business."

Sometime probably in the late 1960s, Gary organized a couples' bowling team. He enjoyed bowling, and he and Matilda bowled regularly.

"We bowled their team, and they beat us all three games," recalled John Vander Wert. "I fussed. The next morning, Gary went early to the office and put signs up…. 'Beware: John may not be in a good mood today.'

"That is the interest he took in people. All business, but he liked to have fun."

Resolving Differences

In 1989, when he was 71, Gary retired from the company, leaving it in the hands of his son, Bob Vermeer, and his daughter, Mary Vermeer Andringa. His oldest son, Stan, earlier had taken a hand at the helm of the company, serving as president from April 1, 1982 through 1986. As company president, Stan was responsible for promoting hydraulics and bringing professionally trained engineers to the company.

As Vermeer Corporation celebrates its sixtieth anniversary in 2008, the company is led by Bob and Mary, who serve as co-chief executive officers. Shareholders include Gary and Matilda, their three children and eight grandchildren, as well as Harry and Bernice's four children and nine grandchildren.

Although Gary retains the role of chairman emeritus of the company's board of directors, Bob serves as chairman of the board and Mary serves as company president. Several other family members as well as outside advisors are also on the board.[6]

The size and complexity of the company and its many and varied products require the full-time leadership that Bob and Mary provide. In the previous era, Gary had remained a farmer who happened to have a very successful manufacturing business. He was never willing to give up the farm; he wanted to travel, fish and hunt, and frequently became involved in church and community activities. "Farming is my number one occupation," Gary told an interviewer in 1982. "I farm more now than I ever did. This business is really a sideline."[7]

As a result, Gary didn't want to waste time at the plant on niceties. At the meetings that he attended only reluctantly, he didn't want to hear people going on about the positive things. Why waste time talking about things going well? "He would put them in their place quickly and knew how to ask about what wasn't going well. He had a sixth sense for that," said Bob.

"He disliked meetings in general—especially during harvest and planting season," said Steve Van Dusseldorp. If he thought the meeting should end, Gary would turn to Bob and Mary: "Are we done here?"

"He was agitated when he had to come to meetings when he wanted to be out farming," said Bob.

When things were going well, Gary delegated. "If things were not going well, he jumped back in with both feet. He delegated because he loved other things that he wanted to do," Bob said.

Sometimes Gary did feel that things weren't going very well. And, true to his pragmatic no-nonsense nature, Gary called the shots as he saw them. In 1976, significant differences of opinion with his brother, Harry, led to Harry's departure from the factory—and a rift in their family relationship. Harry, who had been with the company almost from the very beginning, left to lead Marion County State Bank.

From 1976 to 1982, long-term employee Carl Boat was president of the company, the only non-family member to fill this position. Again, significant differences of opinion led Gary to replace Carl with his son Stan in 1982. Four years later, Stan also left the company amid disagreements.

Those disagreements over business issues, particularly disagreements involving his relatives and the challenges of running the business with a second generation, remain difficult and sensitive issues for the family. By several accounts, Bob has filled the role of peacemaker in the family, and has enabled healing in the relationships. Before Harry's death in 2006, Gary and Harry were on good terms. Carl and Gary, as well as Stan and Gary, also resolved their differences.

Awards and Honors

Over the years, Gary received many awards honoring him and his business. Pella leaders honored him with a Community Service Award in 1977. In 1984, he was named the Iowa Inventor of the Year. In 1986, he was inducted into the Iowa Business Hall of Fame. In 1992, he was inducted into the Junior Achievement Business Hall of Achievement. In 1996, he was inducted into the Construction Equipment Industry Hall of Fame.

The qualities that led to these awards—qualities like innovation, integrity, and stick-to-itiveness—continue to be essential to Vermeer Corporation. Bob and Mary recognize the value of these qualities, as do Mary's son, Jason, and Bob's daughter, Allison, who have joined the business as members of the third generation.

Bob and Mary were named "Entrepreneurs of the Year in Manufacturing" for Iowa and Nebraska in 1998. They also were inducted into the Pella Industry Hall of Fame in 2007. The company received the prestigious

Gary's induction into the Construction Equipment Industry Hall of Fame in 1996 in Las Vegas

The innovative quad track design of the Vermeer RTX1250 tractor increases side-hill stability and floatation in soft or sandy soils.

presidential "E Star" award in 1990 and 1998 for significant growth in export sales. Under Bob and Mary's leadership, many of the company's products— from the groundbreaking Vermeer Navigator horizontal directional drill to the Vermeer RC9120 and RC5120 Mower/Conditioners— continue to win awards for their design and innovation.

"Gary laid the foundation. Gary built a financially strong business with strong values. Then it was up to the next generation. He gave them an opportunity many people don't get—to run a very successful company," said John Vos. "It was a transition to go from Gary's way of thinking, keeping the same core values, and to keep up with the changing times. Stan provided an initial transition, making possible the transition to Bob and Mary. Bob and Mary are doing a good job, one that is appropriate for the twenty-first century."

And, as always, the company continues to search for a better way.

Throughout its sixty years in business, Vermeer Corporation has manufactured hundreds of different products, today more than 125 product models. It has been issued 169 patents, including 31 from other countries. Gary himself has been issued seven patents, including his first patent in 1959 for a stump-cutting apparatus, one in 1973 for a "method and machine for forming a large round bale of a fibrous material," and his most recent, in 1996, for a direct drive system for a baler.

The company now encompasses 1.5 million square feet— more than 33 acres—under roof. It includes seven manufacturing plants and a parts distribution center that annually ships more than 15 million pounds of freight to customers, as

The 75,000-square-foot Global Pavilion includes a large arena, a training center with nine classrooms on two levels, and the Vermeer Museum.

well as the Vermeer Global Pavilion. The 75,000-square-foot Global Pavilion, opened during the company's fiftieth anniversary celebration, provides a state-of-the-art training center that includes nine classrooms on two levels, as well as the Vermeer Museum.

The company processes 150 tons of raw steel and uses 129 miles of weld wire each day. In 2007, with roughly 2,000 employees, sales reached more than $600 million.

Under Bob and Mary's leadership, the company has reorganized around its customers, dividing itself into four market segments:

Underground Installation: Among the products are the company's Navigator horizontal directional drills. These machines were introduced to the market in 1991 and have been a boon to contractors needing to install utilities with minimal surface disturbance.

Environmental Transformation: This includes an exhaustive line of equipment from brush chippers, tub and horizontal grinders, stump cutters, tree spades, and other products used for land clearing, green waste management, and tree care.

Specialty Excavation: In this area, the company seeks to meet the needs of customers involved in road demolition, surface mining, and site preparation with products that include track trenchers, trench compactors, and a Terrain Leveler attachment.

Forage Management: Besides a wide array of balers, the company offers hay handling tools to transport, wrap, and unroll the bales as well as baler options such as bale monitors, bale ejectors, and automatic twine tie systems. Other products include mower-conditioners, mowers, rakes, and rock pickers.

Vermeer Corporation's retail customers represent a far more varied group than the farmers or nurserymen who made up a large share of the customers in Gary's heyday. And the company continues to recognize, as Gary did from the beginning, the importance of innovation and developing new products. The spirit of Gary's entrepreneurship lives on at Vermeer Corporation. Today's engineers may say it differently, but they are always striving to develop a new product that would have led the company founder to say "Hey, I think we have something here."

Gary at six months

3 Family Heritage

My dad bought me a cultivator when I was ten years old—a special one you could steer with your feet. You put horses in the front of it and sat on it. It cultivated one row at a time.

~ Gary Vermeer

In 1856, just five years before the start of the United States Civil War, Gary's great-grandfather, Brant Vermeer, and his wife, Teunetje Krukland Pothoven, emigrated from Mooi Lunteren, a small town near Lunteren and Utrecht in the province of Gelderland, the Netherlands, to the United States.[1]

Although some Dutch people emigrated from the Netherlands because of religious differences, Brant left for economic reasons. He wasn't a poor Dutchman, but he thought life would be better for his children in the United States.

Brant had been a forty-year-old bachelor when he married Teunetje, a widow with one son, Otto. Otto made the trip to America with the couple as did the couple's own children: twins Gerrit and Anthony, who were thirteen at the time, and their younger brother, Hendrick.

Brant Vermeer's home in the Netherlands as it appeared in 1935

They traveled by ship, a difficult trip that took at least a month. After landing in New York, they traveled by train to Iowa City—the farthest west the train went at that time. There they bought oxen, horses, and wagons for the trip overland to Pella.

Roads were rough; streams to be forded were often treacherous, so that traveling was hazardous and slow. The team of oxen was dispatched long before the horses set out, the idea being that all would arrive at the camping place at the same time. But in the evening those traveling with the horses had the camp in readiness when the group traveling with the oxen arrived. On the last lap of the pilgrimage, Hendrick, eleven-year-old son of Brant Vermeer, got lost near Montezuma. Setting out alone in hope of overtaking the group traveling with the oxen, he came to a crossroad and took the wrong trail. He soon discovered he was lost and gripped with fear, he frantically ran all day until he overtook a company of American travelers. The poor lad was unable to communicate his plight to them but one of them, surmising that he belonged to a company of Dutch trekkers and knowing the course of their journey, restored him to his anxious parents.[2]

When the family finally arrived in Pella, Brant bought an eighty-acre tract of land, northeast of Pella. It had a one-room log cabin, in which the family lived for twelve years. They slept in the attic, accessible only by a ladder from the outside of the cabin.

Pioneering Hardships

Life was hard for Brant, his family, and their fellow pioneers. After finding or building a sod hut or log cabin, a colonist-farmer's next job was to turn prairie into farm ground.

> This sod was thick and tough and required a strong plow drawn by six oxen to tear it up. Moreover, it yielded but slowly to the forces of decomposition. Planting corn was done by hand. One man plowed a slight furrow, another dropped three kernels of corn at every place, and a third [man] with a small instrument called a dumper covered the kernels and leveled the soil. To cultivate the corn, a simple machine equipped with three shovels and drawn by one horse was used. Only one row could be finished in one round. Harvesting corn called for the most exhausting efforts of the whole process: five rows, two on each side of the wagon and one under it, were stripped of their ears by human hands and tossed into the wagon box. The heaviest part of the job was discharging the load of corn by shoveling it into the crib. Wheat was cut by means of a cradle and bundled by hand. Thus, only with unremitting toil, all the crops were raised and harvested.[3]

When Brant arrived in Pella, the town had been incorporated only a year. The Reverend (Dominie) Hendrik Pieter Scholte had founded the town in 1847. In the Netherlands, Scholte had been actively involved in the Separatist movement, an effort led by a group of people who didn't want to obey the king's edicts to worship in the State Church. Some of those who seceded were even being imprisoned, and many decided to emigrate.[4]

Brant immigrated when trouble was mounting on several fronts in the United States. In 1856, Iowa was just ten years old, and the state, like the rest of the country, was unsettled. Foremost in many minds at that time was the issue of

The first log cabin where Brant Vermeer lived with his family after they moved to Pella

slavery. Iowa had been admitted to the union as a free state, but just south of its border, Missouri was a slave state. There were cases in which slaves ran away from Missouri masters to Iowa. Some were sent back. Others were protected, and some abolitionists organized a branch of the Underground Railroad through the state.[5] After southern troops captured Charleston's Fort Sumter and started the war, people living in southern Iowa were especially afraid of attack.

Meanwhile, people in northern Iowa worried about Indian attacks. Just across the border, in southwest Minnesota, the Dakota people (also called the Santee Sioux) were engaged in a deadly conflict with settlers, starting in August 1862. Many settlers and Sioux died, and 38 Dakota men were executed en masse in Mankato, Minnesota.[6]

Despite these conflicts, colonists continued to arrive from other countries. In 1860, there were nearly 675,000 people in Iowa, of which more than 100,000 were immigrants. These included Germans, Irish, English, Norwegians, Scotch, Swiss, French, Swedes, Welsh—and more than 2,600 Dutch. Thirty years later, there were more than 300,000 people in Iowa from foreign countries.[7]

Besides the Civil War and Indian wars, colonists also faced the usual worries wrought by bad weather, horse thieves, and epidemics. Cholera hit Pella hard in

1854, and small pox in 1856, the year Brant arrived.[8] Both epidemics were nearly disastrous to business, as was the Panic of 1857 that sent the country into a severe but brief economic depression. "Money was not easy to obtain; employment that brought in cash was hard to get. The boys of Brant Vermeer received only twenty cents for a day's work."[9]

Despite the hardships, Brant persevered, and in 1867, he bought a second farm, this one with 160 acres.[10] Buying farmland would become a tradition passed on to his son Gerrit, his grandson Jacob, and eventually to his great-grandson, Gary Vermeer.

Opting to Stay in Pella

Born October 14, 1843, in the Netherlands, Gerrit was a teenager when he arrived in Pella. His descendents don't know much about his youth, but the adventure of the family's travels and the new life that awaited him in Pella must have been exciting for this young man.

Anxious to learn English, Gerrit opted to attend Sunday School at Second Reformed Church, which used English in its services—even though his family attended First Christian Reformed Church.[11]

He was thirty years old when he married Hendrika De Bruin, twenty-one years old, on April 23, 1874. The couple lived northeast of Pella at first, then moved four miles east of Pella. Finally,

Gerrit Vermeer with his grandson, Gary

in 1882, Gerrit bought a farm two miles east of Pella where he would raise his six children.[12] This farm, designated as a Century Farm in 1982, is part of the Pella Nursery property, and remains in the hands of his descendents. Gerrit's great-great grandson, Josh Vermeer, lives on the property.

Hendrika and Gerrit, a twin himself, had twin daughters, Tonetta and Minnie, who were born December 8, 1874. Bertha came along in 1877, followed by Jacob "JG," who was born on the same day as the twins but eight years later. Jennie was born in October 1884, and their youngest, Mattie, was born in October 1889.

Like his dad and most of his neighbors, Gerrit farmed. A good wheat harvest may have been a pivotal factor in keeping his family in Pella. At one point, Gerrit was set to leave Pella with his two brothers and settle in Orange City, Iowa—home to another large Dutch population. Threshing a bumper crop one day, they discussed options. "You know," said one. "I don't think the wheat will be any better there. Why don't we just stay?"

It's an interesting speculation to contemplate how Pella and Orange City might be different today had the wheat harvest been poor that year.

In 1895, when Hendrika and Gerrit's youngest child, Mattie, was five years old, Hendrika died. She was only forty-five years old. The family had just built a barn, and it being the biggest building available, the family held her funeral there. She was buried at Black Oak Cemetery, just east of Pella. Mattie remembered a train came along during her mother's funeral.

After his wife's death, Gerrit continued to farm. The oldest girls, Minnie and Nettie, helped care for their younger siblings.

Even as the older children left home, Gerrit continued on the family farm with Mattie and Jacob until Jacob got married in 1917. Gerrit and Mattie then moved to town, to a house at 601 Washington Street, which was torn down in 1986 for a city parking lot.[13]

In his later years, Gerrit was the proud owner of a Kissel touring car. Made by the Kissel Motor Car Company of Hartford, Wisconsin, the Kissel car featured an aisle between the front and back seats. Mattie took him for a drive almost every day. He died May 30, 1923, and is buried next to his wife in Black Oak Cemetery.[14] It was not until after his death that Mattie married.

An Ambitious and Enterprising Father

Gary's parents, Jacob and Anna Vermeer, 1917

Jacob, whom the family called JG, was Gerrit and Hendrika's only son. Born December 8, 1882, he lived most of his life on the farm Gerrit had bought two miles east of Pella. JG grew up farming with his dad, and during the winter he broke and trained horses for others throughout the area. He also enjoyed hunting.[15]

Jacob's dad gave land to each of his daughters, but he gave the family farm to his son.

Jacob married Anna Elsie Haven from Grand Rapids, Michigan, whom he had met when she was in Pella visiting a friend. Jacob was thirty-four and Anna was twenty-two when the Rev. J.J. Burggraff married them in the Grand Rapids home of Anna's parents, John and Elsie Wondergem Haven on August 23, 1917. After the wedding, the couple took the train back to Pella and moved into the family home.

Jacob was an ambitious man. Interested in business and law, he obtained a diploma from the Chicago Correspondence School of Law. He was active in his church and in the community. He served as both a deacon and elder of the First Christian Reformed Church. He also served on the boards of several community organizations including the Pella National Bank, Pella Farmers' Coop, and the Plain View country school. Besides his church and community work, Jacob was a hardworking and successful farmer. Even before he married, he was buying additional farmland.

A little more than a year after their wedding, Jacob and Anna's first son, Gary J. Vermeer, was born at home on September 29, 1918. He was baptized Gerrit—named after his grandfather.

Jacob and Anna went on to have three more sons: Elmer H. (Dutch), born June 7, 1920, John H. on May 13, 1925, and Harry G. on March 22, 1929. All were born at home.

Gary has only vague memories of his Haven grandparents. John Haven was a successful architect and contractor in Grand Rapids.[16] Gary recalls one of his grandparents' visits. "It took them three days to get from Grand Rapids to Pella. There were no signs on the road." But his

Gary's maternal grandparents, John and Elsie (Wondergem) Haven were from Grand Rapids, Michigan.

grandparents were able to drive part of the distance along the White Way—one of a limited number of designated highways. Gary remembered, "The fence posts were painted white alongside it to mark it. There once was a White Way Auto Company of Pella, because of the name of that road."

In the fall of 1925, when Gary was seven years old, his family moved into a new home that his dad built. The new home was so close to the old one that the family handed John H., then just an infant, through the windows from the old house to the new one. Jacob bought a Delco generator from Gerrit Vanden Berg, who sold quite a few of them to farmers from his Pella store. The Delco was an engine-driven generator that would charge a whole row of batteries to provide electricity to the house. That provided the family with electricity, and thus, they also had running water from a pump. The family relied on that Delco for its electricity until 1932 when the power company ran electric lines to the house.

Upstairs, Gary remembered, the new house had three bedrooms and a store room. Downstairs, there was one front room, a bedroom, the kitchen, and a bathroom. Gary's parents slept upstairs. There were two boys in each of the other bedrooms. "I still remember lying upstairs trying to take a nap, and the birds were in the tree chirping. I can still hear them chirp."

Learning to Farm and Hunt

When Gary was perhaps ten years old, he came down with appendicitis. Though Dr. Williams, who operated on a table in the family living room, gave him ether to put him under, Gary didn't go under right away. "It was a terrible experience. It felt like my head was going around in a barrel."

After that surgery—perhaps as a reward—Gary's dad bought him an air rifle. A few years later, Gary got his first .410.

Gary, Harry, Dutch, and John, 1929

Hunting—or just shooting—was a regular part of the farm boy's life. In the evening, hawks roosted in two elm trees in the back of one of the fields. "We would go there after dark, look up in the sky and shoot them," Gary remembered. "My brother Elmer [nearly two years younger than Gary] went out to shoot one, too. On the way, he shot a skunk. We didn't believe him, but we checked the next morning, and the skunk was there. We didn't believe him because he was just a kid."

Jacob liked to shoot hawks, too. Once, when he was plowing, he saw a hawk go after a rabbit. Jacob got the gun and shot the hawk. "In those days, hawks would eat chickens so we would shoot them. Nowadays, you're not supposed to," Gary said.

Similarly, farmers had little use for pocket gophers. Gary hunted them on Tone Van Zee's farm. When Tone's son, Gene, was just two years old, he'd watch Gary catching the pocket gophers. "He came out and said, 'Little doggie, little doggie,' when he saw the gophers," Gary remembered.

At that time, the county paid a bounty for the nuisance animals, requiring that hunters furnish proof with two front feet. Gary once took in the front feet from fifty-four gophers. The woman in the Knoxville courthouse started to count them—picking them up gingerly with her fingertips. "After pulling out just a few she stopped and said, 'Oh, I'll just take your word for it.' We got ten cents per gopher. That was big money in those days."

By all accounts, Gary's dad, Jacob, was a hard worker, a good farmer, and well-respected. "Their dad was a wonderful person," said Marsha Overbergen, Gary's cousin and Jacob's niece. "He was kind of quiet. When he talked you always listened. He was interesting and caring. He helped my mother so much. He was a gentle man.

"I remember sitting around their kitchen table," she added. "We had to be quiet when the farm news came on. He wanted to hear those markets that came on at noon on WHO [radio]. When he wanted to hear the markets, we knew to be quiet."

And Jacob was never without his pipe. "My dad had a pipe in his mouth all the time," said Gary. "He walked with a pipe in his mouth."

Anna, Gary's mother, was a serious woman, a bit stern even, and a good pianist. Raised in Grand Rapids, Michigan, as the daughter of a successful architect, Anna must have found the move to a small rural farming community a significant adjustment. Her sons remember her as a good mother who took good care of them. "In winter time, they had somebody over every week," Gary remembered. "I'd come home from school, and I'd smell that chocolate cake."

"Their mother was kind of sickly, not real healthy," said Marsha. "She doctored in Des Moines. I remember when John and Dutch would take her to Des Moines to the doctor, and we would go along. We thought it was a big thrill. We ate at Bishop's Cafeteria."

Because of Anna's health problems, Dutch helped with the cooking, and later, after Dutch was out of the house, Harry helped his mother.

"When Dutch got home from the service, I called him one time, and he was cleaning the wallpaper in his mother's living room," said Dutch's widow, "Jay" Vermeer. "I thought, 'My goodness, here is a guy who has been a captain in the army, was part of the Normandy invasion, and his mother has him on a ladder, cleaning wallpaper.' But he didn't say no to her."

Another person who influenced the boys was Aunt Mattie, Jacob's youngest sister. For a while after she married, Mattie Jansen and her family lived on a farm about a mile north of Gary and his brothers. Gary remembers that the Vermeer boys were her favorites.

Aunt Mattie, Aunt Net and Aunt Jennie, 1958

The boys sometimes took the horse and buggy and visited Aunt Mattie. "We would go in the barn and catch the pigeons that were almost ready to fly, young ones. And she would make pigeon soup," said Gary. "We wouldn't eat it the same day. It was too close to the live pigeon."

Most of the boys' lives growing up revolved around the farm. As the oldest, Gary probably shouldered a fair amount of responsibility, although with four boys in the family, he shared the workload.

Jacob, who didn't particularly like to milk cows, started Gary early on that chore, probably around age ten. The family milked two cows—just for their household use. Gary remembered, "Once in a while they would kick their foot in the bucket—milk wasn't as clean as nowadays. But I am still alive. It didn't seem to hurt us any."

Anna made butter, and the family sold the extra cream if they had any. Jacob took the cream and eggs into town to the co-op grocery store and got credit that he used to buy other groceries.

Often chores around the farm made it hard for Jacob to find time to get to town. "Uncle Jake was so busy on the farm, he would call in his grocery list," remembered Marsha Overbergen, who by that time had moved with her mother, Mattie Jansen, into town. "We would get them from the store. He would come to our house long after the store was closed and get the groceries from our house."

Gary's dad settled up at the grocery store once a year—a day Gary always wanted to accompany his dad into town. On that day, Gary's dad received a cigar and Gary got a candy bar— both complimentary. Gary said, "When you only got it once a year, a candy bar was a big deal."

Besides the milk cows, the family had the usual farm animals. Although the family named their animals, Gary always saw them more as work animals than pets. There were the four brown Belgian horses: Lark, Bess, Ginger and Daisy, and the two mules: Jack and Jerry. Although Jacob had a tractor as early as 1922, the family still relied on the horses for most of the work. The tractor was used just for plowing.

Use of horses or mules, and the number of each, depended on the job. To disc and harrow, they used four horses. When they cultivated, they needed two horses to lead the cultivator. Two horses also led the manure spreader. "I hauled a lot of manure with horses," Gary recalled. "We'd shovel it on the wagon and go out to the field and spread it.

"I remember when Dad and I cultivated corn, and mother would bring out coffeetime. When the horses would see her coming they would speed up because they could rest at the end of the row.

"Mules were more ornery," Gary continued. "We had some that would run away once in a while. I had a team of mules who ran one on each side of a tree with the harness between them. They had lost the wagon by that time."

As a young boy, Gary was ready to farm, holding the reigns for Lark and Bess.

Besides the crops, Gary's dad raised cattle and hogs, and briefly, even some sheep. Jacob usually had about seventy-five head of cattle and some stock cows and calves. He bought the calves in the spring—when they weighed about 400 pounds—and sold them just after Thanksgiving at about 1,100 pounds. Jacob hired trucks to transport the cattle, six or eight at a time, to the John Morrell and Company's meat packing plant in Ottumwa, about forty miles to the southeast. Gary remembers going along once in the 1928 Chevy to weigh them. He about froze to death, he said. He had a piece of cherry pie in Ottumwa that cost fifteen cents.

Another time, Jacob shipped cattle to Chicago to sell. Gary went with his dad to Chicago by train to see the sale.

The family also raised Leghorn white chickens. "They would run all over the yard. They would lay eggs in different places, and you would have to find them."

Regarding pets, there were a few cats around the farm. The family also had a tan dog, Carlo. "My brother and I would go and drown out ground squirrels [from their holes], and the dog would go wild. Carlo would have one before it got out of the hole. When you got out the bucket of water, the dog would just go crazy."

Though some farm boys dream of leaving the farm when they grow up, Gary didn't. He liked farming. Gary remembered going out to the field with his dad as one of his favorite pastimes.

But Gary never has been particularly introspective and has never explicitly articulated why the farm has always been such a draw for him. He is interested in history, particularly family history, so part of the reason may have been tradition. Farming was how he grew up. He learned it from his dad, who learned it from his dad, who learned it from his dad.

Gary, too, has always liked being outside and farming gave him a reason—even while at the factory—to get outside. Gary is also a practical man, a man who likes to see tangible results. Farming certainly fit the bill there, too.

And the tinkerer inside him was drawn to the technology advancements of his time. As a young man, probably before he married, he debated on WHO radio the benefits of the horse versus tractor power.[17] He witnessed the coming of the tractor and much more. It fascinated him.

"We used to pick corn by hand," said Gary. "It would take three to four hours to pick a load of corn. About ten o'clock, you would get on the yard with a load of corn. Then [in 1939] my dad bought a one-row corn picker. I went out early in the morning, and when the sun came up, I had a load of corn already. I thought that was unbelievable!"[18]

Still another draw for Gary was something less tangible: the sights, the smells and the sounds of farming.

"I would still like to go out there and hear those bangboards. Of course, farms were a lot closer together then. You would go out early morning, and if it was real quiet you could hear all around you the corn hit the bangboards, and then you'd hear it drop on the floor. And then after a while you wouldn't hear it. You had a thirty-six-inch high wagon box and an additional three or four sideboards on the other side, and so you would throw the corn against there and hear it bang and it would drop into the wagon."

It would be easy to paint a nostalgic picture of Gary's farm life, but it involved a lot of hard, hot, and dusty work.

Threshing was usually one of those hot and dusty chores. July—which can be very hot and humid in Iowa—was the time to shock oats and thresh. Neighbors got together and went from one farm to the next to thresh. Uncle Art Van Donselaar took care of the threshing machine. Gary, already obviously mechanically inclined, took over when Art retired.

Sometimes, no matter how hard one worked, other forces took control. The summer of 1934, for example, was dry and incredibly hot. The crop was very poor that year, and cinch bugs—tiny pests, maybe a quarter of an inch long—by the millions ate what little crop there was, sparing no one, including the Vermeer family, that year.

Schoolboy Escapades

Gary, 4 years old, on his way to school

Along with his brothers, Gary attended a country school, Plain View School, from first through eighth grade. Gary and his brothers walked 1 ½ miles to school, carrying their lunch in a bucket, sometimes a Karo Syrup can or perhaps a tobacco can.

There were three in his class when Gary started school. When he graduated, there were two. In fact, there were only about twenty students in the whole school, and one teacher: Janet Steenhoek. "She taught us what we ought to know. In first grade you were already learning eighth grade stuff because you heard them recite. That wasn't all bad."

The one-room school was heated by a coal and wood furnace in the basement. Most desks were one piece with tops that flipped up to reveal a storage area for books.

One day in school, fellow student Ralph Bogaards excitedly pointed above the teacher. "The school was on fire," recalled Gary. "The teacher got us out, and we went to the neighbors. They got the fire department and saved the school."

There was also excitement the day Miss Steenhoek caught some of the older boys—Gary included—smoking corn silk near the creek north of the school. It was fall, and the boys had stuffed the dried silk into a pipe and smoked it. The teacher grabbed a twelve-inch wooden ruler to crack across the boys' hands. It

The Vermeer boys attended Plain View School. In this 1929 photo, Gary is in the second row, fourth from left. His brother, Elmer, is in the second row, second from left.

broke over Ralph Carrico, the first one she hit, Gary recalled, allowing the others to escape the physical punishment.

Observing that incident made an impression on Gary's brother, John, too. "I was four, and I didn't break a rule for four years!"

That wasn't the only time Gary smoked. He and Tudor Vermeer, a distant cousin and a fun-loving boy four years older than Gary, snuck some of Jacob's King Edward Cigars out of the cellar one day and smoked them in the cattle bunks. They smoked until they got sick. Gary got so sick that he vomited, but his parents never asked about it—though they must have smelled the cigar smoke on him. "I never tried smoking after that. Our sons never cared to smoke either."

Although there was more than enough work on the farm, Gary and his brothers and friends knew how to make their own fun.

The boys played softball, sometimes in a field near Plain View School, other times in a field nearby with the neighbors. They had a purchased ball and bat, but makeshift bases. "We used anything we could find for bases, sometimes pinned burlap. That wasn't real important. Sometimes, we just marked it," said John.

Gary often hung out with Anthony Vermeer, who lived nearby. "I did quite a bit of hunting with Anthony," said Gary. "We shot lots of rabbits one time, but they were sick so we didn't eat them. I would spend the whole day at Anthony's."

In the winter, the boys went sledding. There was an especially good hill to the north of the school.

With neighbor Gary Gezel, Gary once made a kind of go-cart that he christened a "scrambola." It was powered by a Montgomery Ward 1.5 horsepower gas engine his dad had used to pump water before the family got electricity. The engine powered one of the four wheels that the boys had borrowed from a cultivator. Though it ran reasonably well and could carry the boys over the fields, they had to push it up the hills because it didn't have enough power.

A few times, the family went to Des Moines—especially when Grandma Haven visited from Grand Rapids. They went downtown to Younkers and ate at Bishop's Cafeteria.[19] Other times, the family went to the Iowa State Fair in Des Moines where Gary especially liked watching the planes fly over the stadium. It was there at the fair that he and his brothers watched rodeo performers standing and riding on their barebacked horses, which gave the boys a similar idea. "We tried it, and it wasn't as hard as you thought it would be," said Gary.

Like a lot of boys his age, Gary had a mischievous side to him. At a church Young People's picnic, he and some other boys caught a bull snake. "We had the girls sit there and close their eyes, and we laid the bull snake across their laps. We got quite a reaction from them! It was kind of a dirty trick."

It seemed that Gary's mischievous side was especially apt to come out when he got together with his friend, Anthony.

Some nights, the boys tied a piece of iron to a gutter. Then they tied a kite string to the iron, walked way out into a field, and pulled the kite string causing the iron to bang against the gutter. "Pretty soon, the lights would come on, and people would come out," said Gary, laughing again at the memory. "But we had it high enough that they would walk under it. When they would get back in the house, we would pull it again."[20]

Another time, Gary made a cannon from a piece of gas pipe. "We pounded dynamite powder in there and put a fuse on it," said John. "That sure woke up the neighbors early."[21]

Other times, Gary and his brothers tied a rope onto a tire pump or even a tire and put it out on the road. People drove by, and when they noticed it, they backed up to take a better look—but the boys by that time had yanked the object off the road. "We had a lot of fun," Gary said, "and it didn't cost much."

Not costing much was important. The family wasn't poor; still, they weren't about to waste what they had—especially in those times.

Gary had just turned eleven when, in October 1929, the stock market crashed. Although the depression had less impact on self-reliant farmers than urban people, it still made a deep and lasting impression.

Ever the farmer, Gary remembers what it did to prices. "Corn produced sixty bushels an acre, and at ten cents a bushel, you got six dollars and the taxes were six dollars. So there wasn't any way you could make any money."[22]

His dad, who had quite a bit of land even before he married, owned at least five farms when the depression hit. He didn't lose any of them. Jacob rented out some of the farms, and personally farmed 200 acres.

"My dad was a pretty good businessman," said Gary. "When Pella National Bank went broke in 1932, they named him supervisor. He would tell me a lot of things to do and not to do in business."

One farm Jacob owned a few miles south of Pella was used by the Diamond Block Coal Company. The Vander Zyls mined that coal, perhaps for as long as ten years, starting in the mid-1930s. Like many people in the area, Gary drove a wagon led by a team of mules to the mine to get coal.

"The mules didn't like it at all in that hole. It was an open mine, and you could drive right down there with a wagon. They had fellows down there loading the coal. There were probably about twenty people in there mining that coal. They would dynamite it and then load it by hand into the wagon," Gary said. "We dumped the coal into the coal chute on the west side of our house."

Everybody bought coal in those days to heat their homes. The coal wasn't good quality; it had a lot of sulfur in it. But because local coal was easier to get, people still bought it.

Jacob sometimes got as much as $1,000 per month coal royalty. "My dad had no problem during the depression because of the coal mine," Gary said.

After graduating from Plain View School, Gary went on to Pella High School where there were fifty-three in his class when he graduated in 1935. Gary, who has always enjoyed learning his family history, found the history as taught by Miss Jane Gosselink to be particularly interesting. But he also liked math, taught by Miss Ver Heul, and physics, taught by John Groenendyk.

He thought all his teachers were good ones, and he liked school. Though Gary went to class only half-days his senior year so that he could help his dad on the farm, he was on the honor roll.

There wasn't much in the way of extracurricular activities in those days, or much time for the farm boys to participate—but Gary did find time to act in one or two school plays. He couldn't have known then, but those plays must have impacted him later, both as a director of plays, and as a man who often would take center stage in other ways in his adult years.

Jacob and Anna's Final Years

In the mid-1930s when he was in his early 50s, Jacob started having significant health problems. He was sick for about a year—though neither John nor Gary know from what—and wasn't able to do as much farming after that. Although the family hired men to help on the farm, Gary, just sixteen at the time, started assuming more responsibility. Gary worked on the farm six years, and when he married, John started working on the farm.

John, who received the family farm, married in 1949. After John's marriage, Jacob and Anna moved to 507 Washington Street in Pella, where Jacob died on January 15, 1952, just a month past his sixty-ninth birthday. Gary believes his dad had Alzheimer's. "They called it hardening of the arteries in those days. He would walk around town and get lost."

Gary's parents, Jacob and Anna Vermeer

Two years after Jacob's death, Anna moved into a smaller house at 806 West First Street. She still maintained a close relationship with girlhood friends in Grand Rapids as well as newer friends she had made in Pella, according to daughter-in-law Jay Vermeer. And, as she had always been, she was firm in her faith. "She lived it," recalled another daughter-in-law, Bernice Vermeer. "She didn't want to miss Ladies Aid. She let us know that she was a Christian, and we had to live by it."

Anna, however, sometimes played favorites, which was fine as long as you were one of her favorites as was granddaughter Mary Ann Vermeer Andringa, who was named after her grandmother.

"I have a lot of good memories of her, but not all cousins do. She could be demanding," said Mary. "Once a year, she would take the cousins to Des Moines for the whole day. That was a big outing for us. We would go early in the morning. We would first go to Walgreen's and she would buy us something, but the big thing was lunch at the Younkers tea room, often when there was a fashion show.

"We loved it. It was a huge deal for us," Mary added. "One or two of the mothers may have gone along, but the focus was on the granddaughters. Grandma grew up in Grand Rapids and had loved the city. So she loved the city of Des Moines, too."

Anna died at the age of seventy-eight on May 2, 1974.

Brothers Branch Out

From left, Gary and Matilda, Elmer and Jeannette, John and Effie, and Harry and Bernice

After high school, Gary's brother, Elmer (Dutch), attended Central College for two years and Calvin College for one year before enlisting in the army in 1941. He graduated from officer's training school as a Second Lieutenant and in January 1944, volunteered and joined the Second Ranger Battalion as its demolitions officer in Bude, England. He made the landing at Pointe du Hoc on the Normandy Coast on D-Day, June 6, 1944, with the Rangers and was awarded the Silver Star.

After the service, Dutch farmed and served in the Iowa House of Representatives for five terms and as Speaker Pro Tem in 1957. He also for many years served as an administrative assistant to Iowa Gov. Robert Ray. Dutch married Jeannette "Jay" Lankelma in 1946, and they have five children. He died in 1989. [23]

After graduating from Pella High School in 1942, Gary's brother, John, worked on the family farm until 1946. He then farmed with his brother, Elmer, for a couple years. On February 8, 1949, he married Effie De Jong, and they had three children.

John was always interested in growing things, which he attributed to a crop of peanuts that he planted and harvested as a youth. In 1960, John, Dutch, and Earl L. Pohlmann founded Pella Nursery. John went on to serve as president of the Iowa Nurserymen's Association and president of the Iowa Fruit and Vegetable Growers Association, and has been active in many other community and church leadership roles. He lived for many years on the family farm that his grandfather Gerrit had first purchased, and now lives with his wife in Pella.[24]

The youngest of the brothers, Harry, went to Calvin College for 2½ years, taking a pre-seminary course and active on the debate team. In January 1950, he left college to work at Vermeer Manufacturing Company. In February 1951, Harry was drafted and spent two years with the Forty-Seventh Infantry Division in Camp Rucker, Alabama. On November 23, 1951, he married Bernice Tromp, and they had four children.[25]

After the service, Harry went back to Vermeer Manufacturing Company and served as vice-president, secretary, and treasurer. He left the company in the mid-1970s and bought out Gary and Ralph Vermeer's stock in Marion County State Bank, where he became chairman of the board. Harry was active in his church and community and served in many leadership roles in both, including two terms on the Pella City Council. Harry died in 2006.

Van Gorp Heritage

About three miles down the road from where Gary lived with his parents and brothers was the 120-acre farm that belonged to Matilda's parents: John M. Van Gorp and his wife, the former Minnie Blom.

Matilda's grandparents, Engel and Tunitje (Van Zee) Blom immigrated to the United States before Matilda's mother, Minnie, was born. Pictured left to right: Bert, Arie, Tunitje (widowed), Minnie, Antonie, and Edward.

Born in 1886, John was the son of Marinus and Gertrude (Van Roekel) Van Gorp. He had two sisters and three brothers, in addition to a brother who died in infancy.

Minnie, born in 1889, was a first-generation American. Her parents, Engel and Tunitje (Van Zee) Blom, had been born in Holland, as was her older brother, Arie. In 1900, Engel died of pneumonia, leaving Tunitje a widow with four children and pregnant with their fifth child. The four boys helped Tunitje work the farm, and Minnie quit school to stay home and work.

No one knows how Minnie and John met, but they married October 17, 1912. Their first child, Gertrude, was born in 1915, followed by Edward in 1918, Matilda in 1920, Evelena in 1925, and John Jr. in 1930.

The Van Gorp home, five miles east of Pella, was a typical two-story farmhouse with three bedrooms. Like the Vermeers, the Van Gorps had electricity from Delco batteries charged by an engine during the day. The children slept in the two small bedrooms upstairs—the girls in one room and the boys in the other.

In Search of a Better Way
The Lives and Legacies of Gary and Matilda Vermeer
103

While Gary's father was an astute and assertive businessman who knew how to invest his time and money, John Van Gorp's attitude toward money was more laid-back. Even though his own family's finances were tight, he was apt to share it generously with other families he thought might need it more.

In 1934, a year that was terribly hot and dry, the family's horses died of "sleeping sickness," and the hogs died, too. "I do not remember Dad complaining about it," said Evelena. "Mom was a little more antsy. She worked terribly hard."

Matilda's family was poorer than Gary's, and their lives sometimes were quite hard. Money was often scarce. The family didn't have indoor plumbing, and used a second-floor chamber pot at night. "I didn't have an inside toilet until we married. Gary put it in in the fall," said Matilda. "That was one thing that was not much fun when it was cold. You would have to go outdoors to the toilet when it was so mighty cold."

While food was plentiful, the family worked hard for it. The family took cream and eggs into town and traded for groceries, paying the cash difference each time. In winter, the Van Gorps took their eggs and cream to town on a sled pulled by horses. "It was interesting, but I wouldn't care to do it again," said Matilda.

Matilda, like all her siblings, helped around the farm as soon as she was old enough. She milked cows, fed and cleaned chickens, worked in the family's large garden and helped with the cooking and sewing. She also canned vegetables, beef, and pork with her mother.

Minnie taught Matilda to sew. "Mother did a lot of sewing and baking. Life was so different then. She worked hard. It makes me feel bad when I think how hard she had to work.

The Van Gorp family: (front row, from left) Minnie, John Jr., John, Matilda. Back row, Evelena, Edward, Gertrude

"My mother and grandmother didn't have a lot. Grandma Blom was a widow for many years and also had to work hard," Matilda added. "My dad was always so satisfied. Money didn't mean anything to him."

Despite their father's easy-going nature, Matilda and her brother both recall being a bit frightened of him as youngsters. "Dad told the truth, and he didn't beat around the bush," said John Jr. "I would never dare lie to him because he thought lying was just terrible. I would always tell the truth."

Though the work was hard, Matilda doesn't have any regrets about her simple and frugal youth, which she believes has made her satisfied with the small things in life. "I think you inherit that, and I am thankful for it. I am just as happy as anyone who lives any other way."

Matilda was ten when John Jr. was born, an event that took her totally by surprise. "I thought my mother was changing shape and sitting quite a bit more, but I didn't know he was going to be born. We heard him crying in the morning."

She was happy about it, and was just the right age to play mother to her brother. "She really babied me," John said. "She was a good sister. She took good care of me.

"I remember sledding in the snow in the moonlight with Matilda," he added. "I was five or six; she was fifteen or sixteen. We went sledding on the lane. It was a good coasting hill."

His memories of her, even when they were older, still are good ones. "Sunday afternoon, I would go out and chore with my dad and brother, and when I would come back in the house, she would be sitting by the piano, singing and playing hymns, old-fashioned hymns—sometimes with Evelena, but most times by herself. It's a pleasant memory."

Although memories of the family's childhood games are dim, Matilda remembers the family's rope swing that hung from a tree in the yard. It had a board seat for the children to sit on. "Once I thought I was so smart, and I climbed the rope. I let myself slide down, and boy, did I have sore hands!

"We also played in the pasture. It had a creek. We weren't supposed to play in it, but we did."

She also recalls a time when she went hunting. Sort of.

"We used to have owls sitting in the trees a lot. We often sat on the lawn in hot weather. My brothers got the gun, and I said, 'Let me see if I can shoot him,'" Matilda recalled. "Ed stood behind me in case the kickback was too strong, and I would fall. But I didn't. And two owls fell out of the tree! I must have been about twelve or so. I don't think I have ever shot a gun since."

Matilda's dad hated driving, so her older brother, Ed, started driving the family's 1926 Chevy when he was eleven. He didn't need a license in those days. Though Ed didn't want Matilda to drive it, she drove it anyway, up and down the lane.

Matilda went to Wheat Grow country school, but of all the Van Gorp siblings, Matilda's sister, Evelena, was the only one who went to high school. According to Evelena, the only reason her dad let her go was because Pella Christian High School had started at that time.

In grade school, Matilda and Evelena milked the cows before breakfast, then walked a mile to catch a ride to school. "Dad brought us with a buggy when it was muddy," said Matilda. "I always enjoyed watching the wheels go through where the horses walked. They would make a ridge between where the horses walked."

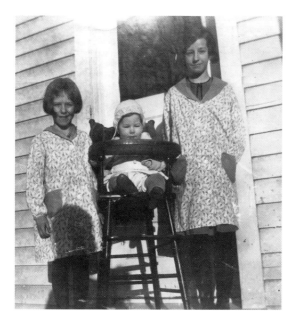

Matilda (on right) and Evelena wear the smocks they wore over their clothes to school as they watch over their brother John.

The two girls wore smocks over their school dresses—a common practice at the time—to protect their dresses. Minnie made them each two, which would get them through a week. The smocks then would be washed and good for another week. "It saved your dress," Matilda explained. "It didn't get as dirty, and it lasted longer."

As always, money was tight. So when Matilda had the opportunity to earn some money, the occasion stuck in her memory. In third or fourth grade, Matilda got a special treat when she swept the floor for the teacher, earning ten cents for her work. "I could buy two boxes of Cracker Jacks for that."

Another job came along when she was about thirteen years old. Matilda and her cousin Leona cleaned the house of an aunt who was sickly. "'Did you clean the lights?' she would ask. We worked there all week. When we left, our folks picked us up, and we each got fifty cents."

Matilda has few photos of herself during her teen years. "It was the Depression, and we didn't own a camera. A sitting with a photographer was too expensive." Pictured, front to back, are: John, Evelena, Matilda, and Gertrude.

It wasn't much even then for a whole week's worth of work. "But that was okay," Matilda said, "they didn't have money either. My aunt made pudding out of skim milk her son brought from the farm. I didn't like it. It's crazy that you remember those silly things."

One highlight for Matilda and a lot of Pella residents at the time was the big mission festival, held every year in West Market Park. Missionaries from all around the world visited Pella then and told the gathered crowds about their experiences.

"Going to mission fest was a big deal," said Matilda. "When we went to mission fest, we would each get a dime. We could buy two things for it. I thought that was pretty nice."

Although Matilda was more interested in visiting with her friends than listening to the missionaries, the church was a big part of her life. Every Sunday, morning and evening, the family went to church. As a young teenager, Matilda memorized a certain number of Bible verses and received a Psalter from the church.

Mealtimes in the Van Gorp household were always opened with silent prayer and ended with Bible readings. "My dad never prayed out loud," said John Jr. But the Bible readings happened morning, noon, and night without fail. "My dad never missed."

"I remember reading a verse in Dutch," said Evelena. "Dad would read the Bible in Dutch and give us kids a chance to read a verse in Dutch."

In fact, Matilda and her siblings grew up speaking both Dutch and English in the home. Grandma Tunitje never did learn to speak English, although she could understand it. And Matilda's own parents spoke Dutch at home for a long time. "When John started school, he couldn't speak much English," Matilda said. "I don't think the rest of us had a problem with that."

In 1946, Minnie had her first bout with cancer. For a short while, she rallied, and Minnie and John made a trip to Denver—"the big trip of her life," Evelena recalled. But the cancer—she had both ovarian and colon cancer—returned. She died in 1950. She was sixty-one that year.

After his wife's death, John lived for a while with his son, John Jr., then divided his time among all his children after John Jr. married.

"He was a very tender-hearted man, a kind man," said his grandson, Bob Vermeer. "He grieved the death of his wife for a long time. I can still picture him sitting smoking a cigar in our living room." He also shared Bob's interest in horses. "He loved to go to sale barns. He and I went together—to the Pella sale barn, and to the Oskaloosa and Colfax sale barns. The first horse we bought was Ruby. The next one was Babe. He went along to pick out both of them."

Mary remembers that Grandpa Van Gorp often lived with them in the winter time. "He was a very gentle man who often spoke Dutch. He never wanted to be in the way. He was such a dear man. He was like my mom. Often he had candy in his pocket." John Sr. died in 1968 at eighty-two years old.

Courtship Begins

Matilda was two years younger than Gary and went to a different school, but she did attend the same church: First Christian Reformed Church of Pella. In 1934, Matilda's Sunday School class was just across the sanctuary from Gary's class when he noticed her, though they both were too young to date. "I don't remember a thing the Sunday School teacher said, but I remember seeing her."[26]

Gary Vermeer, 1935

Gary went on to graduate from high school in 1935, and joined his dad farming. When he was farming next to the road, he sometimes saw Matilda drive past in her family's open touring car. He waved. She waved back. "I thought someday I would ask her for a date, but I didn't have any opportunity."[27]

Then came a particular Sunday in July 1936, a day that was so hot Gary's parents decided to forego church attendance that evening. Gary went alone. Seizing the opportunity, Gary asked Matilda to take her home from church that night. She said yes. Matilda was 16; Gary was 17½.

Teenaged Matilda with brother John, 1937

That started a tradition. Every Sunday night after church, the couple dropped Gary's parents off at home, then went on to Matilda's house. At first, Gary drove a dark blue 1928 Chevy with a trunk on the back; later his dad bought a 1937 Chevy.

Matilda's house was about a quarter-mile down a lane from the main road. Lacking gravel, the lane was often muddy. During those times, Gary parked the car, and the couple walked the lane to her house.

Going home from church together was about all that the courting couple did. They may have gone to the church's Young People's Society occasionally, but usually they just went home to Matilda's house. Her parents went to bed and left them to themselves. One of Matilda's siblings, also dating at the time, courted in an adjacent room. Gary always left at 11:30 because he had to be home by midnight.

One Sunday, the snow was so heavy and blowing so hard that the Van Gorps didn't make it to church, Matilda recalled. "But then on Sunday night, who comes plowing through?" She gestured toward Gary. "This guy!"[28]

Another time, Matilda remembers that when Gary asked her for a date, she answered that she didn't know. Characteristically, he didn't like that. "Say it," he told her. "'You have to give me an answer one way or another.' He didn't like indecision."

The two families shared the same religious values, and Matilda's family liked the Vermeers. "My dad thought a lot of Jake Vermeer. He thought he was a smart man."

Neither of them had ever dated anyone else before, so what drew them together? In recent years as they reminisced over their courtship, Matilda in her genuine, self-effacing manner said that Gary must have married her for love because she wasn't blessed with looks or money.

Gary, on the other hand, answered in his own characteristic fashion. "I didn't have any other choice. The other girls didn't want me."

After 3½ years of dating, Gary decided around Christmastime in 1939 that it was time to get married. His mother helped him pick out the diamond at Wilson's Jewelry in Pella. They paid $25 for it. "When we bought that diamond, we had to go sit in a separate room so other people didn't see it," Gary remembers. He gave Matilda the ring at Christmas 1939.

*Matilda with Stan, born in 1942,
and Bob, born in 1944*

In Search of a Better Way
The Lives and Legacies of Gary and Matilda Vermeer
113

4 Family Living

My wife and I had heard of couples who didn't get along very well. I heard my folks talk once about a couple who fought like cats and dogs. I didn't think that was any good either. We both had some questions about whether we would get along well.

One night we made a covenant. In my lifetime, I have made hundreds of agreements and signed lots of contracts, but this is the most important one I ever made. We agreed that no matter what happened we would always try to make the other person happy. I want to say that Matilda has always done that. I hope I've done as well as she did. We've had a wonderful fifty years together.

- Gary Vermeer, Fiftieth Wedding Anniversary Speech

On Valentine's Day 1941, Gary Vermeer married Matilda Van Gorp. It was Matilda's twenty-first birthday.

They married in a simple ceremony in the living room of the home of Matilda's parents, who lived five miles east of Pella. Besides the immediate families, only a few aunts and uncles—perhaps thirty family members altogether—bore witness to the small afternoon wedding. Matilda wore a navy dress with white trim; Gary, a business suit.

Gary and Matilda, Feb. 14, 1941

Afterwards, the family shared chicken sandwiches, angel food cake, and ice cream. That evening, when a few people arrived to shivaree the new couple, Matilda was thankful they were a tame bunch. "Our shivaree-ers didn't do any naughty things like they did at some weddings."

That first night, Gary and Matilda stayed with Matilda's family. For the next two weeks, they lived with Gary's parents before they went to their own home on the farm Gary's dad had bought for them east of Pella. As was typical with rental agreements then, the farm had been rented out for a year that ended on February 28. Gary and Matilda moved into their new home on March 1, the day after the renters had left.

Starting a Farm and Family

Gary has always been proud that he and Matilda started their life together free of debt. Besides the house, Gary's dad gave them 120 acres surrounding it. According to Gary, Jacob Vermeer also gave his son $2,000 for the five years that Gary worked for him. Gary used it to buy cattle, hogs, a car, and enough equipment to start farming.

Matilda's dad gave them some chickens and two cows—a good milk cow named Star, and another cow named Beauty. Her parents also set them up with some furniture—a davenport and a bed—as well as pots, pans, and dishes for the kitchen.

For the first years of their marriage, Gary and Matilda lived off the income from the farm. "Gary always said if you couldn't make money after World War II, you weren't much of a farmer," said his oldest son, Stan.

Gary planted corn and soybeans on their 120 acres. That first year, he harvested one hundred bushels an acre on his ground—a bumper crop considering his family had only been able to get eighty-five bushels per acre previously. (Gary's dad had owned sixty of those acres long before Gary and Matilda's marriage.)

Wartime price controls kept corn prices stable those first few years, but by the late 1940s, prices fluctuated greatly. In 1946, corn prices rose nationally to a season average of $1.53 a bushel. Poor planting conditions in much of the country caused prices to rise again in 1947 to $2.16 a bushel, but by 1948, prices fell nationally to $1.28 with some areas seeing prices below $1.00 per bushel.[1]

The young couple's income was relatively small, but so were their expenses. Star provided them with milk each day. The chickens gave them their breakfast each morning. They also took eggs and cream into town and exchanged them for groceries. Other income came from cattle and hogs.

They butchered their own hogs and cattle, usually in the winter. Matilda was familiar with the process. Her father had been a butcher before he married. She froze some of the meat, which they ate over the next few weeks. The rest she steamed and canned.

All in all, it was a simple and tranquil farm life, exactly what Matilda expected when she married. "Gary was frugal when we got married. It didn't bother me because I was used to it."

Gary and Matilda with Stan. The proud parents are standing in front of Matilda's family's home, where they married.

On November 4, 1942, their first son, Stanley James, was born at home. "There was gas rationing when Stan was born, so Gary thought he could be born at home," said Matilda. "It didn't go as easy as Gary thought, so the other two were born in the hospital."

Stan was born with the cord around his neck, and Matilda was thankful for the midwife, Mrs. Frank De Jong, who helped with the delivery. "She was a dear old lady. Well, I guess she wasn't that old, but she seemed that way to me at the time." After the delivery, Matilda stayed in bed ten days, as was typical of new mothers in the 1940s.

"Grandpa Vermeer was very proud when he had a grandson, and we were proud, too, when we had Stanley," said Matilda.

When Stan was born, Matilda first learned that Gary had reoccurring problems with a rapid heartbeat. Gary was in bed about that same time for about ten days, too. He consulted a doctor in Des Moines who prescribed some medication that helped, although throughout his life he continued to experience an occasional rapid heartbeat, which required him to take pills and rest until it subsided.

At four weeks old, Stan still wasn't yet up to his birth weight. "One Sunday, Gary stayed home so I could go to church," Matilda recalled, an occasion that has stuck in her memory probably because it was so unusual. "I came home, and he said, 'It took three diapers to clean him up!' We didn't have disposable diapers and wipes in those days."

One morning soon after that, Matilda went down to the basement to fire up the furnace, her early morning routine. "We had a furnace, and there was a big round hole in the middle of the floor where the heat came up through. It was the only heat, except for the cook stove," Gary explained. "She would get up with the baby and fire up the furnace."

That particular day, Matilda first noticed some of their eggs that had been stored in the basement had been eaten. Then she saw a little animal walk over a partition. It was what Iowans called a civet cat—others might know it better as a spotted skunk.[2] Gary set a box trap, with a long rope attached, and put eggs in it. "It wasn't very long and I had him." Gary pulled the critter out into the orchard and got rid of him.

Gary took it in stride. "We had lots of mice in the basement, too. My folks always did, too. It didn't bother me any."

Nearly twenty-one months after Stan was born, Robert Lee came into the world on July 28, 1944, in the Oskaloosa hospital. Five years later, on November 22, 1949, Mary Ann was born—just a few weeks after Bob and Stan had the measles.

"They were pretty happy when they got a sister," said Matilda. The family didn't have a television, so they read a lot, which the children really enjoyed. "When Mary was little, she would crawl somewhere and get into mischief. It made Stan angry because I had to quit reading."

On a windy November day in 1953, when Mary was four years old, the family moved to a new house immediately south of their first home. That home, at 1688

In this 1953 photo from the Pella Chronicle, *the Vermeer's old house is moved to town.*

Adams Avenue, is where Gary and Matilda still live in 2008. The old house was moved to Jefferson Street in Pella, where it remained in use until it was torn down around 2005.

Martin (Bats) De Jong, a local carpenter who fifteen years later would become Bob's father-in-law, designed and built the new house. It had four bedrooms, one bathroom, and no basement. De Jong's daughter, Lois Vermeer, said this was because Gary didn't want one. It would hold too much stuff, he said. "He was Lean already, before Lean became popular."[3]

Gary, however, said they didn't have a basement because Matilda didn't like the dirt and uninvited animals in the basement in their old house. Probably both stories have merit. In any event, Matilda, a young mother, had little to do with the design and construction of their new home. The whole house cost $28,000 including drapes and carpeting.

Just before Christmas in 1954, when Mary was five years old, the Vermeers added another member to their family after their neighbor, Leta Mae Van Wyk, contracted polio, paralyzing her from the waist down. Leta Mae was six months pregnant when she got sick and deeply concerned about who would care for the baby. Her mother was already elderly.

"I asked Gary if he cared if we took her," said Matilda. "I like babies. He said okay."

So when Cheryl Van Wyk was just five days old, the Vermeers drove to Des Moines to pick her up at the hospital.

"She was different from our kids. She was not a good sleeper and didn't wake up happy," said Matilda. Even so, the family quickly became attached to the new baby. She had wonderfully curly hair, and the kids loved her.

The Vermeers kept Cheryl for eleven months. "People were sure I was going to have another baby after Cheryl left," Matilda said. "I knew all the time I couldn't keep her. I can see how people who adopt children love them. We knew this all along, but you still miss them."

Learning Life's Lessons

Gary never was one to be idle, and by the late 1940s and into the 1950s, he found himself facing increasing demands for his time. The fledgling factory, started in 1948, required his attention. So did many other activities. By the late 1940s, he was taking flying lessons and by the 1950s, he had become very active in church and community.

Despite these time demands on Gary, there was one thing Matilda wasn't about to budge on: dinner time. As a farm wife she had dinner ready at 11:15 a.m.— because his folks did that. "But he came home an hour later than that from the factory sometimes. That got to me. 'If you are a business man, you can't just leave,' he told me. I told him, 'You have to just do as the boss says.'

From then on, Gary made sure he was home on time for dinner.

With Gary frequently gone, Matilda took the responsibility of caring for the children and having food on the table, a typical arrangement for the 1950s. "I taught the children a lot more than he did. But he taught them to be honest and so forth.

"They said you mustn't spank kids, but I did," said Matilda. "But you could just set Bob on a chair and look at him and that was enough." Usually.

Matilda tells the story: "I used to go to Ladies Aid Society in the afternoon. You went to so much work in those days. I had put clean clothes and white shoes and socks on Bob. He was upset about something, and so he stepped in a mud puddle in a track in the yard. Dutch was there, and he thought it was so funny. I didn't think it was so funny because I had to change Bob. I didn't spank him often because he was so tenderhearted, but I think I did this time."

By the mid-fifties, the factory was bringing in enough income for Gary and Matilda to live comfortably. And they did change their lives somewhat: Gary bought more land for farming and hunting, the family traveled more frequently and for greater distances, and, at the suggestion of banker Glenn Andreas, Gary joined brother Harry and cousin Ralph to set up a charitable foundation. All these changes can be attributed to the increasing income the factory provided. Nevertheless, the family's day-to-day lives changed little. The values Gary and Matilda learned in church and growing up in the depression were too ingrained to change their lifestyle now. Those were the same values they continued to impart to their children.

"I did not teach them that money was the most important thing," said Matilda. "We never talked about money. It still doesn't mean much to me. I am thankful I can give it away."

With the exception of their travels, the Vermeers continued to live their simple, rural lifestyle. "When Mary was in college and had to fill out college forms, she asked Stan if Gary was worth $30,000 or not. She had no idea," said Matilda. "Stan told us about that. He got a kick out of it. He knew better because he was seven years older."

Like many wives of her era, Matilda was on a budget for groceries, clothes, and other household necessities. "Five hundred dollars didn't go so far for a month for utilities, clothes, groceries, donations, and all of that," she recalled. She didn't even consider getting an automatic dishwasher until the mid-seventies. "The kids wanted me to get one. They said, 'Mom, you have to get one.' I didn't use it a lot at first. I don't mind doing dishes, and you always have to do the pots and pans anyway. I really didn't use it much until the past two years or so. I still do the pots and pans by hand."

Later, when Stan's bicycle was stolen when he was in college, he got another bike. Gary didn't offer to give him a car.

Stan, Mary, and Bob are ready for Tulip Time.

Matilda always took care of domestic bills. "As soon as I get a bill, I pay it right away. I am afraid I will lose it or something."

She has never been comfortable handling funds or accounting for them. "I don't like working with figures. I was treasurer for the high school auxiliary and it wasn't my cup of tea at all… Stan would help me with the books, making it come out right. Gary says just keep good track— what you spend and what you get in."

As children, the Vermeers were interested in the usual things. Growing up in Pella where the annual Tulip Time festival and accompanying Dutch parades loom large in community life, Stan was fascinated with floats. He made one from an orange crate mounted on the back of a red wagon. Mary was his queen.

Stan also liked making electrical things. For his fourth birthday one year, he asked for supplies to make a light. He was independent and inquisitive. "I had a mousetrap on a ledge going down into the basement. I said, 'Don't touch that!' and sure enough, he did," Matilda recalled.[4]

The three children loved their pets.

As a farm family, they had an assortment of farm animals and pets—a dog and plenty of cats. When one of their sows had too many piglets, the family bottle-fed four of the babies. When the family had to bottle-feed a lamb, it became so tame that it greeted Gary every morning when he stepped out the door. When the lamb grew into a big sheep the family could no longer keep, it was difficult for Bob, who was fond of animals.[5]

Though Bob loved all animals, he took a special interest in horses and once had a pony that was growing unusually fat. A vet assured the family that she wasn't pregnant, but one morning Bob was happy to discover their not-pregnant mare had given birth.

Despite the family story about Bob calling Stan a "dirty old skunka rat"—a term he made up in a moment of irritation—most of the time, the boys played well together, according to Matilda. Indoors, they played with an erector set, Lincoln Logs, and a train. Outside, the boys liked jumping off a platform, which they had built in a tree, while holding onto a tire swing. They also made tunnels out of square bales to climb through. Sometimes they went to their uncle's home—John H. Vermeer's home—after school to watch TV because the family didn't have one of their own.[6] "Sometimes they would sit by a building—and just sit there talking," Matilda said.

Mary loved dolls. "She had a bunch of them. She played Sunday School with them, and I don't know what else," said Matilda. Grandma Vermeer—who was thrilled to have her first granddaughter—always bought Mary a doll every Christmas and birthday. "When Gary went away on business, he used to buy Mary a little doll," said Matilda.[7]

Gary with Mary

"Mary was a good baby because she sucked her thumb," Matilda remembered. "She sucked that thumb so hard that she put a crack in it."[8]

For several years, Matilda and neighbor Ella Menninga took their four sons to swimming lessons. "We didn't realize how privileged we were in learning how to swim, because not many kids our age learned how to swim," said Stan.[9]

With Dutch domestic prudence, Ella and Matilda shared an electric hair clipper. "We cut our boys' hair until they went to high school," Matilda said. "We each kept the clipper for a week, passing it back and forth. I only cut Gary's hair once. It made me so nervous, I didn't ever do it again."

The family rarely ate out. "We would only go out to eat on Mom's birthday and their anniversary. I always had a hot beef sandwich with gravy and mashed potatoes," Stan recalled. Once, though, when they returned from Matilda's birthday dinner, they discovered a new 1956 Chevy in the garage. Gary had arranged for someone to put this surprise birthday gift there while the family was gone.[10]

As would be expected of Gary and Matilda's children, Stan, Bob, and Mary had chores to do—mostly helping around the house and farm. Stan helped butcher chickens. Bob milked Buttermilk, the cow. They all helped in the garden that provided the family with beans, peas, potatoes, onions, carrots, radishes, lettuce, and strawberries. They also picked apples, cherries, and peaches from their orchard. Matilda regularly canned the produce. "I'm sure I canned 100 jars of peaches one summer."[11]

Gary's day-to-day involvement with his young family was significantly less than Matilda's. Self-motivated, Gary always expected the people around him to be likewise—whether they were his employees or his children. He wasn't a father who often encouraged or complimented his children. Instead, he provided them opportunities.

"He gave assignments, and said, 'You can do it,'" Stan recalled. As the children grew older, they naturally took on more responsibilities.

One summer, Gary provided Stan with an hydraulic scaffold on the front of a tractor and told him to paint the barns. Another time, when he was a teenager,

Stan helped put in clay bell tiles at the camp. He took one from the wrong place, the pile rolled, and half-dozen of the tiles broke. "He did not get angry about that," Stan remembered.

Stan also remembers stacking hay bales in the barn, which was hot and dusty work. Bob remembers helping out around the farm, walking the beans, putting up the hay in the summer—frequently under the tutelage of the farm manager.

Faithful in Worship and Living

For many Pella residents, it would be easy to take for granted the role faith has played in the Vermeer family. As home to a large Dutch Calvinist community for whom the church has always been an integral part of life, Pella has more than two dozen churches. About half of these are part of the Dutch-influenced Reformed and Christian Reformed denominations. Even more than 160 years after Pella was founded by Rev. (Dominie) Hendrik Pieter Scholte and 800 other Dutch colonists, one of the first questions asked of newcomers is "What church do you go to?"

But as part of a country where only forty percent of Americans claim to attend church regularly—quite-likely the actual number is substantially lower[12]—the Vermeers are in the minority. Even more rare is that their faith did not simply require Sunday worship, but was something Gary and Matilda daily instilled in their children.

"I wanted them to be honest. The most important thing is to be a Christian and live that way. Love others," said Matilda. "I loved them and prayed for them and with them. I helped them with their catechism and Sunday School lessons."

Gary's interest in his children's faith lives became more evident as the children became older. As a youth leader in his church, Gary broke from tradition and willingly led his children and other youths in discussions about subjects they wanted to talk about, Mary recalled. "As a leader he was open to discussing movies and dating."

Gary with his three young children

"He asked good questions and challenged young people with what they really believed," added Bob. "Biblical principles were always important to him. He enjoyed discussing theology and values. Stan, Mary, and I were taught to carry those out practically."

Sometimes, as youth leader, Gary directed his own children in plays. Mary remembers going along to play practice and on tours. Matilda did the makeup. When Bob and Stan were in a play about two little rascals, they took the play on the road, Mary recalled, to Western Christian High School in Hull, Iowa, as well as to the nearer Iowa towns of Sully, Oskaloosa, and Prairie City.

Stan, Bob, and Mary also learned from their parents as role models. At church, the children watched both parents actively participate in the services and church organizations. At home, they observed their parents taking regular part in Bible studies and theological discussions, and hosting missionaries. The children learned the importance of faith.

In more recent years, Gary and Matilda's faith has borne witness to their grandchildren, particularly at family dinners on Sundays. "Grandpa always prayed before the meal," granddaughter Heidi Quist remembered. Afterwards, either Grandpa or Grandma read some scripture, and the other read a devotional out of the *Today* series. Then they closed in prayer. "There was a clear reverence they communicated to us."

Hopping the Plane

When Mary was just a few months old, Gary got his pilot's license and launched his life-long love for travel.

Matilda's favorite vacations were the ones with all three children along. "We did that a lot in the summer when Gary flew. He would have to make a business call somewhere, and the kids would go along. That was a really fun time."

Every year, the family explored a new place. In 1957, the family went to a Billy Graham crusade in New York City; Stan especially remembered thirteen-year-old Bob's response to the altar call. "He wanted to go forward. Mom and Dad wouldn't let him."

In 1958, Gary flew the family in his plane to California. That was the time the family dinged a rental car in Yosemite Park on one of the park's winding roads.

Gary often took his family along when he flew to business meetings.

During a 1960 trip with the Bonanza to Alaska, Gary took the family aloft to see the sun at midnight. The family also climbed a hill to try to see Mount McKinley, which at 20,320 feet is the highest peak in North America. "Bob and I had more stamina, and we got higher, but we never did see the peak," Stan recalled. On that same trip, Gary flew by himself to Point Barrow, the northernmost point of the United States, while Matilda and the children went to a fort near Fairbanks, Alaska.

Flying back from Alaska to Pella, Gary was forced to stay behind a storm front. He decided to follow the Alaska Highway so he could land his single-engine plane on the road if necessary. "It was bad weather. We couldn't fly over or under it. We had to be able to see the highway," said Stan. They were forced to make overnight stops en route home. The trip to Alaska took one day from Edmonton; the trip back required three.

"We waited many times at airports for the weather," said Gary. "They didn't have all the stuff they have now. Matilda would watch for railroads and towns when we flew."

Family Time at the Camp

A property four miles northeast of Pella known affectionately as "The Camp" by the family, is also familiar to many of their friends and acquaintances.

Initially purchased as a hunting ground, the camp has become an icon for Gary and Matilda's simple and generous lifestyle. Here, they successfully blended their love of farming, hunting, and activity with their love for family, their concern for church and community, and their desire to provide new experiences for all.

The camp is not the resort of a millionaire. It is the investment of a hunter, farmer, father, and community man. Every tillable acre of land is planted with either corn or beans. The duck blind and the piping system to flood the lake were built for hunting. The dock and boats—shared liberally—are for family and community pleasure.

Gary bought the property in the early 1960s from his hunting buddy, John Vande Noord, who had bought the camp area himself in the early 1940s from the Maytag Company. When John owned it, Gary lent him a pump to fill the lake with water. In return, John let Gary hunt ducks and geese there.

As one would expect from a place owned by the Vermeers, the camp is practical, and useful, but eminently simple and plain. There are three small buildings and two lakes on a couple hundred acres of land.

Family members, hunters, church members, and many others have enjoyed good times at Gary's camp near Pella.

The buildings include a storage shed, a shower house, and a small cabin with brown siding and wood steps. Inside the cabin, off a small entryway is a bathroom. The entryway leads directly into the kitchen with a coffeemaker on the counter and two wooden welcome signs on the wall. Off the kitchen is a meeting room like one would expect to see for church retreats. Carpeted with a dark, utilitarian carpet, the room includes long folding tables, folding chairs, a leather recliner, and a TV. The wood-paneled wall displays a few of Gary's hunting trophies—deer, elk, moose, and fish. A few stuffed duck, geese and other fowl perch on a shelf.

Outside the cabin, large trees shade two nearby picnic tables. A thirty-acre lake is just across the driveway. On the bank overlooking the lake are three swings—a tall swing for adults or older children, a swing set appropriate for younger children, and a bench swing for the older generation. Nearby is a cracked cement pad with two poles, ready for a volleyball net.

After the Vermeers bought the camp, Bats De Jong—the same man who built their house—asked Gary if he could relocate his boat to that lake. Gary consented, and that is how water skiing started there.

On summer evenings when the family had nothing else that needed to be done, Gary and Matilda gathered up the children and headed for the camp. "We never had any problem with them going anywhere they shouldn't. They loved to water ski," said Matilda. "Our kids didn't have to drive miles to do things."

"I remember spending every night there in the summer," said Mary. "We had hamburgers at nine o'clock, after we had skied."

When the in-laws came along, they, too, joined in the camp fun—one activity after another. "The family didn't sit around and visit," said Mary's husband, Dale. "They were always doing things. It always revolved around doing things, rather than visiting."

"When we finish eating, it is time to go play volleyball. We can't just sit and chat," said Bob's wife, Lois. Smiling, she added, "We in-laws have managed to drag them down a little. We are always walking about ten paces behind."

Even so, Lois learned to water ski there. "Gary taught me how to water ski—along with hundreds of people. He would stand in the muck or drive the boat relentlessly until finally it would happen."

When the grandchildren came along, Gary taught them to water ski as well. Even into their seventies, Gary and Matilda were still water skiing.

It's now the great-grandchildren's turn to become familiar with the camp. Because Gary and Matilda's home isn't large enough to accommodate the growing family, the family is apt to meet at the camp for special occasions. At these times, now in their later years, Gary sits in the recliner in the corner and Matilda soon pulls up a chair next to him. "And they'll watch the pandemonium," said Granddaughter Christy. "It's really chaotic with the kids and grandkids and the great-grandkids."

Drawing Others Into the Family's Camp

Gary's family often gathered at the camp for special times. Here, Gary's mother and brothers and their families pose for a photo in the early 1960s.

As much as the family loves and enjoys the camp, it never was a retreat, at least not in the withdrawal sense of the word. The opposite is closer to the truth. Matilda's family, John H. Vermeer's family, and other extended family members sometimes gather there. And again, Gary, wanting to create new experiences for people, initiated other gatherings.

Gary taught many people to water ski on this lake by his camp.

"Why don't you grab a couple steaks and some potato salad and join us at the lake?" Gary often asked his neighbors on Saturday afternoons. Kent Ver Meer, a neighbor whose father was a distant cousin of Gary's, remembers such conversations happening frequently. They went on Saturdays, after the chores were done, about 6:30. It was a special opportunity for Iowa farm kids to water ski. Kent recalled, "Anytime he had something fun to share, he'd share."

Kent remembers a particular day at the camp, a day when "I knew everything just like every thirteen-year-old does." That inherent cockiness led him to ask if he could try out Gary's new water ski—a banana ski, which Kent described as a wide ski like a snowboard but one that he soon discovered was extremely hard to control because it had no rudder underneath to keep it going straight.

Though others may have felt some wariness about Kent's request, or at least may have felt some obligation to warn him, Gary felt no such need. "Sure, go ahead," he told Kent. Gary took him out to the part of the lake where they customarily skied, revved up the boat, and took off, towing Kent behind. "I'm hanging on, looking like a keystone cop on this thing, slipping and sliding."

Kent made it around two times and almost a third before he lost it. "I hit the water between 30 and 300 miles per hour. I never could do a cartwheel before that, but that day I did five of them in five seconds."

When Gary pulled up alongside Kent to make sure he was okay, Kent apologized for wiping out. "Are you kidding?" Gary told him. "That's a new record. No one has made it around three times." Kent was astounded. "That was Gary; he was that kind of a guy. He liked a good joke."

As Kent started to climb back into the boat for the customary ride back to shore, Gary told him, "You're a Vermeer. You skied out here, and you'll ski back." When they rejoined the others, Gary announced Kent's success with just two words: "Three times."

At least weekly, the Vermeers hosted factory employees at the camp for a night of burgers or steaks, volleyball, and water skiing. Quite often, they showed slides from vacations usually featuring animals that Gary found fascinating, such as wildebeests from Africa or penguins from Antarctica.

Other times, the Vermeers invited people experiencing tough times, such as a death in the family. Several people remember the Vermeers inviting groups of widows for a meal. Granddaughter Mindi, for instance, has memories of her grandpa having a great time with a group of widows one evening. "I remember him loving it and playing all these games."

The Vermeers often played games with visitors, games such as "scissors." In this game, everyone sits in a circle taking turns handing off a pair of scissors while saying either "the scissors are crossed" or "the scissors are uncrossed." Each person makes all sorts of adjustments to the scissors but only those in-the-know understand that the determining factor is actually whether your legs are crossed or uncrossed when you pass the scissors. "We had so much fun with that game," Matilda remembered. "We acted like it was all in the scissors. That was kind of a dirty trick, wasn't it?"

Youth groups were also frequent guests at the camp. Providing a night of skiing, volleyball, and hamburgers was evidence of Gary and Matilda's interest in them. Even today, the Vermeers continue to permit youth groups to use the facility.

A Special Place for Music

The family sings to Gary and Matilda at their 50th wedding anniversary celebration.

When Gary and Matilda celebrated their fiftieth wedding anniversary in 1991, their children hosted other family and friends at a celebration in the auditorium of the Pella Opera House. As part of the presentation, the children and grandchildren sang one of Matilda's favorite hymns, "I'd Rather Have Jesus," and Gary's favorite hymn, "Living for Jesus." They also sang one of Gary's favorite songs from *The Sound of Music*: "Edelweiss."

To everyone blessed to hear them, it was evident the family enjoys musical talents. Matilda, in her natural unassuming way, attributes the family talent to Gary's side of the family. His mother, Anna Haven Vermeer, was a good pianist.

But Matilda herself grew up with music in her household. Her mother taught her to play "Jesus, Lover of My Soul" on a pump organ.

After the pedals on her family's pump organ wore out, Matilda's family got a piano. For a while on Saturdays growing up, Matilda took lessons.

Matilda enjoyed playing the piano most of her life.

"Before I was married, on Sunday afternoons, we played and sang some hymns," said Matilda. "But I didn't continue that with my kids. Our kids were nappers on Sunday afternoon."

She has always liked to sing and for a time even sang in choir at Calvary Christian Reformed Church.

For Matilda, it was the hymns that were special. "Gary and Matilda would come over to our house in town along with Gary's brothers for a meal," recalled Marsha Overbergen, Gary's cousin. "Afterwards, Matilda would play the piano and we would sing. Matilda had a nice voice. We sang our favorite hymns. I always thought Gary was so proud of her because she played so well."

The hymns continue to hold a special place in Matilda's heart. "We bought a little CD player and every night we play a CD with hymns. They are just like I learned, and they are so wonderful to me," Matilda said. "And I think Gary likes it, too." Matilda still occasionally plays hymns for her own enjoyment on the family spinet piano.

Gary and Matilda's three children share a love for music. All three sing and have played instruments. Many of the grandchildren, too, share their musical talent. Granddaughter Heidi, for instance, majored in vocal performance in college, a talent she continues to put to use in her church.

Stan and Family

The year that Gary flew his family to Alaska, 1960, Stan graduated from Pella Christian High School. Generally a serious student, Stan enjoyed his classes. He sang in the school choir two years and played trumpet four years in various bands throughout his high school years.

During summers, he worked on the farm, and used some of the factory's prototype machines in the fields.[13] Over Christmas break his senior year, he worked on the hay crusher assembly line at the factory. The following summer, he worked in the experimental department with Arnie Mathes, a valued employee of Gary's.

Following high school, Stan headed for Calvin College, a school located in Grand Rapids, Michigan, which is affiliated with the Christian Reformed Church.

For two summers during college, he participated in his church's Summer Workshop in Missions (SWIM) program in California. In 1964, he graduated with majors in English literature and mathematics.

Stan wasn't sure what he wanted to do after graduation, but in his senior year he heard someone talking about a great experience teaching in Japan. Intrigued, he talked it over with his parents and with the mission board of his church, expressing his desire for a year's assignment teaching in a place where English was spoken. There were two options available: in Nigeria or in Australia.

As a result, after graduation, Stan spent a year teaching at the Mkar Teachers Training College in Nigeria—an experience that convinced him to enter seminary. The following year, he studied Hebrew in Jerusalem at the Hebrew University of Jerusalem and at the American Institute of Holy Land Studies before entering Calvin Seminary in 1966.

Stan and Margaret, July 22, 1968

Two years later, he married Margaret De Boer, a teacher and a native of Grand Forks, North Dakota. In the fall of 1969 they both headed to Nigeria, teaching among the Tiv people at Bristow Secondary School in Gboko, Nigeria.[14] Gary and Matilda's first grandchild, Christina Joy, was born on July 13, 1970 She was a month premature and spent her first month in an incubator in Jos, Nigeria.

In 1974, while pregnant for the second time, Margaret discovered she had cancer. The couple returned to Iowa for treatment, and Jonathan Gary was born on June 11, 1974. For a while, Margaret's health rallied, but in 1978, she died. Margaret's illness and death was a difficult time for Stan and their children, but their faith provided comfort and courage.

Stan and Alma, January 5, 1980

Over Labor Day weekend in 1979, Stan met Alma Lee Verdon, who had acquired an education degree in consumer science and was working in Wichita, Kansas, for the Navigators—a Christian evangelical organization. A mutual acquaintance said that she felt led by the Lord to pray for a wife for Stan and helped arrange the meeting between Stan and Alma. "It was like a blind date," said Alma. "We believed that God had put us together." The couple married on January 5, 1980. Two years later, on March 12, 1982, David Stanley was born.

Stan had begun to work at Vermeer in 1975, initially in the ag experimental department with Arnie Mathes. In 1979, he started in the industrial experimental area and then, late in 1981, began doing marketing research. In 1982, he took over the presidency for four years, and then left and founded his own engineering company, Pella Engineering and Research. Still living in his rural home with Alma north of Pella, Stan spends his time studying and writing and also is involved in missions and philanthropy work. His wife, Alma, enjoys cooking and is active in outreach ministries for her church.

Daughter Christina (Christy) is a 1993 graduate of Wheaton College in Wheaton, Illinois, where she earned bachelor's degrees in political science and

Stan's family, 2008

business/economics. She also earned a master's degree in information systems from Colorado Technical University in 1996. She lives in Colorado Springs, Colorado, where she works in her own scrapbooking business.

Son Jonathan obtained a communications degree in 1996 from Wheaton College. A writer making his way in the entertainment industry in Los Angeles, Jonathan enjoys tennis and soccer and loves traveling, camping, backpacking, and outdoor adventure sports like mountaineering, kayaking, sailing, and rock climbing.

Their youngest son, David, attended Wheaton College for two years and then transferred to Dordt College in Sioux Center, Iowa, where he graduated in 2004 with a degree in chemistry. He lives at home, working with his father.

Bob and Family

When Bob was in high school, he played intramural sports and was involved with music, singing in various choirs, as well as singing in a male quartet and playing sax in the band. Like his older brother, he often worked on the family farms, especially over the summers. He also tried out prototypes from the factory, such as the hay crusher.

Bob joined the Vermeer construction crew one summer to build the roller rink and Dutch Buffet east of Pella that his father helped finance. Other summers during high school and college, he worked at the factory, in the machine shop, assembly area, and office.

After his high school graduation in 1962, Bob attended Dordt College for two years. Closely associated with the Christian Reformed Church, Dordt is located in Sioux Center, Iowa, and at that time only offered two-year degrees. There, Bob sang first tenor as a member of an elite acappella choir. Interested in economics and business, Bob transferred to Pella's Central College, graduating in 1966.

After graduation, he worked for Marion County State Bank for eight years, getting a good education into the workings of a small and rapidly growing bank by working in bookkeeping, in the teller line, in loans and other areas until he became a vice president and a member of the board of directors. After many years of being away from the bank, he once again joined the board of directors in 2007.

Bob and Lois, June 6, 1968

Bob also spent six months on active duty in the National Guard after college graduation, first working as a medic while stationed in Texas and then later as part of a military police unit.

In 1974, he joined Vermeer in accounting and finance. In 1982, he became vice president of finance. He now serves the company as Chief Executive Officer—a role he shares with his sister Mary—and is also chairman of the board.

During Bob's tenure at the bank, he married Lois De Jong on June 6, 1968. Though Lois was a Pella

In Search of a Better Way
The Lives and Legacies of Gary and Matilda Vermeer
141

native whom Bob knew, the couple didn't start dating until 1965. Lois taught fourth grade at Pella Christian Grade School before becoming a stay-at-home mom. She serves as executive secretary of the Vermeer Charitable Foundation.

Bob's family, 2008

Their first child, Daniel Robert, was born on July 24, 1970, just eleven days after Dan's cousin, Christy, was born. Dan, who grew up to share his grandfather's passion for hunting, teaches history and coaches at Pella Christian High School. He and his wife, Tricia, have four children: Brant, born in 1996; Isaac, born in 1999; Jack, born in 2002; and Ella, born in 2005.

Bob and Lois had their first daughter, Heidi Lynn, on April Fool's Day in 1974, about two months before her cousin, Jonathan, was born. Heidi is a 1996 graduate of Calvin College with bachelor's degrees in psychology and vocal performance, and earned her doctorate in clinical psychology from Wheaton College Graduate School in 2002. Music continues to be her primary hobby, whether it is singing, songwriting, or playing guitar and French horn. A licensed clinical psychologist for Pine Rest Des Moines Clinic, she is married to Chad Quist. They have a son, Alexander (Xander) born in 2004, and a daughter, Anna Louise, born September 23, 2007.

Bob and Lois's youngest daughter, Allison Marie, was born January 6, 1981. Allison, who grew to share her father's love for horses, spent ten years showing horses, earning two world championship titles. A graduate of Calvin College,

Allison obtained an MBA from Drake University in Des Moines. Married to Kyle Van Wyngarden, Allison was a senior financial analyst at Principal Financial in the Des Moines area until the summer of 2007, when she joined Vermeer as industrial distribution manager.

Mary and Family

The youngest of the family, Mary graduated from Pella Christian High School in 1968. An outgoing teenager, Mary became involved in lots of activities in high school. She sang metzo soprano in school choirs, played the lead role in two musicals, was a cheerleader for two years, and performed in plays and speech contests. She also was an attendant on Pella's Tulip Time Court, a long-standing Pella tradition and honor. When she got her pilot's license in high school, she flew her court to meet the Tulip Court in Orange City, another Iowa town that celebrates the Dutch tradition.

Mary and Dale, May 29, 1971

Though she at first considered nursing or a related medical field, Mary opted to study music after high school. Like her brother Stan, Mary attended Michigan's Calvin College and graduated in December 1971 with a degree in music education.

The previous May, while still in college, she married Dale Andringa, a native of Orange City, Iowa, who also was attending Calvin. When she graduated, Mary moved with Dale to Iowa City where Dale entered medical school and Mary taught music and kindergarten in the Iowa City Public Schools.

In 1976, the couple moved to Omaha where Dale served his residency. There, Mary directed a pre-school, taught pre-school classes, and performed in downtown Omaha with a chamber choir. Later, Mary continued to use her musical talent by directing children and adult musicals in churches, especially when her children were young. In 1979, the couple moved to Des Moines. On January 1, 1982, Mary started working part-time for Vermeer doing marketing research and now serves as co-chief executive officer and president.

While Mary and Dale were still in Iowa City, their son Jason was born on September 29, 1975. Jason, whom some of his cousins contend is the grandchild most like Gary, was born on his grandfather's fifty-seventh birthday.

Jason doesn't mind the comparison. "I must be like him because my parents used to call me 'little Gary.' When I get my mind set on something, I won't change it. I'm stubborn, but if I say I'm going to get something done by the end of the day, I will."

Jason holds a mechanical engineering degree from Calvin College (1999) as well as a master's degree in aeronautics and astronautics from the Massachusetts Institute of Technology (2001) and an MBA from the University of Southern California (2005). He and his wife, Carrie, have two children: Danny, born in 2003, and Mia, born in 2006.

Mary's family, 2007

Jason worked as a segment manager at Vermeer Corporation, and in the spring of 2008, he moved to the Netherlands as managing director of Vermeer EMEA (Europe, Middle East, and Africa).

Mary and Dale's daughter, Mindi, was born March 22, 1978. Mindi played point guard at Pella Christian and later at Calvin College, where she graduated in 2000 with a degree in business/communication. Mindi, completing her MBA through Davenport University in Grand Rapids, Michigan, moved from Grand Rapids to Pella in 2008 with her husband, Frank Vanden Bosch. She gained work experience at Cascade Manufacturing and also in banking before the birth of their twins: Jakob and Madeline, born in January 2007.

Through Matilda's Eyes

When Matilda married in 1941, she thought she was marrying a good farmer. But seven years into their marriage, Gary started the factory. "He disappointed me," Matilda said in 2007, probably only partially in jest as she reflected on those early days. She liked being a farmer's wife. It was a life she knew and understood.

"It was disappointing because then we had a hired man to do the farming. Harold Van Maanen was the first hired man. When he got married, the next year, we had another guy who was drunk part of the time. We got rid of him," said Matilda. "It wasn't as pleasant because I had always enjoyed the farm."

Certainly, there were plenty of positives: The business provided the family the opportunity to travel and the opportunity to be generous in the community. It has provided an income and a career path for three generations of Vermeers. It opened Gary's eyes to the joy of flying, and literally took the family throughout the world.

But Gary's dissensions with family or friends at the factory were hard on Matilda, as were the economic downturns.

"There were tough times in the company. Matilda would sometimes say, 'I wish he had never started the factory.' She would have been happy being a farm wife. She sees it as much as a burden as a positive," said Dale Andringa.

Becoming the wife of the owner of a multi-million-dollar company was a significant change for a woman who had envisioned a farming life. Some may believe it is overstating the case to say that the factory thrust Matilda's family into the public eye, but assuredly, the close-knit Pella community started looking at the family with more curiosity than they otherwise would have. Matilda and her children learned to speak carefully, mindful of the weight their words carry and aware that an offhand comment might be misinterpreted and cause hard feelings. Matilda, especially, became cautious, not just out of concern that her words might be misinterpreted and reflect poorly on the family, but her Christian spirit became concerned that her words might be misinterpreted and unintentionally hurt others.

Without exception and with heartfelt admiration, those who know Matilda credit her with living with continual humility and a willingness to serve—an attitude they say is responsible not just for the success of her marriage and family, but also in part, for the success of the company:

> "Part of the reason behind Gary's success was because he had Matilda to cover on so many fronts so he could focus on the company," said Bob Vermeer.

> "Her support and dependability made it possible for him to do a lot of things he wouldn't otherwise have done," said Dale Andringa.

"Matilda has tempered him so much…He needed someone of Matilda's sociability to carry on life. That has served him very well," said Lois Vermeer. "He would not have been successful if she had not been holding the family together all of those years."

"He survives by her. She's amazing and takes such good care of him," said Jonathan Vermeer.

"Grandpa couldn't do a thing without Grandma. They've always been very close," said David Vermeer. "Grandma fills in Grandpa's inadequacies."

"They have such a complementary relationship. She's more a social, emotional-type person, and he's more logical, a business-type person," said Heidi Quist.

On trips to Canada, Gary wanted Matilda to go along even when she would prefer to be home, according to Dale Andringa. "It was not a male bonding ritual. It was not just so she could cook. She was truly a helpmate. She could run circles around people doing work. She was putting fish on stringers, baiting the hook. The joke is that is why he always wanted her to go along. She was sort of the manager."

Matilda organized the food and planned the list when they sought supplies, and generally served as the logistics expert. Meanwhile, Gary was fixing a motor or figuring out how to make something work better on an inflatable boat. "They had their roles. Neither would have been very effective without the other," said Dale.

Her relationship with Gary is an obviously loving one. "She is a servant, a caretaker," said her daughter-in-law Alma Vermeer. "She says her father was always very giving and serving, and she is like him. Gary and Matilda are very affectionate—often holding hands. And I think Gary is quite often the initiator of that."

Matilda and Grandson David are ready for Tulip Time.

That the couple still holds hands isn't lost on their grandchildren either. They've noticed their grandparents holding hands while sitting on a couch, or have seen Matilda's hand lie casually on Gary's arm or leg. In an endearing tribute during their fiftieth wedding anniversary celebration, Gary described Matilda as "a wonderful mother and the greatest grandmother in the world. You know how I know all this? I married her."

In her relationship with Gary, she is probably more assertive than many realize. "Don't underestimate her input into his decision making. Publicly, she plays the dutiful, traditional farm wife from the era from which she came," said Dale. "She has a lot more influence on his decision making than people realize. Gary knows when to defer to her. It is a much more equitable partnership than it is perceived. However, Matilda is comfortable with being perceived as playing a traditional role."

Always productive, always willing to serve, Matilda has another role in the family: the family connector. Alma, who came into the family in 1980, said that Matilda reached out to welcome her. From the beginning, for instance, Matilda sent her birthday cards that said, "We love you," something very meaningful to Alma.

 Unprompted and in separate interviews, at least three grandchildren described Matilda as "the glue that holds the family together."

Grandma sent postcards when away on trips. Christy figures her grandmother wrote to her once a month in college, as she probably did to all the grandkids. Matilda writes even now a few times a year, and calls her once a month or so. "It's never a very long conversation," maybe only five minutes, Christy said. And Gary comes to the phone only if Matilda calls him.

Gary in His Family

Gary connects with his family through activities. Christy, Gary, Brant, and Bob surround a tree at the Woody Place, a wooded property Gary owns north of Pella used for hunting and family gatherings.

Like Matilda, Gary was always active, always productive, and—in his own way—a connector. After all, he invested a great deal of time and money by hosting friends, employees, and acquaintances in his Pella camp and in his Canada cabin.

That's how Gary reaches out and brings his family together—with fishing, water skiing, volleyball, or vacationing. "Early on in our marriage, he asked Mary and me to go with him and Matilda, hiking the Grand Canyon. That was their idea of a vacation. No resort, pool and tan, reading a good book, but a hike all the way down the canyon," Dale recalled. "A safari is grueling, and they were there with the whole family. That has been a role model for Mary and for me, where people are doing things together rather than everyone going their separate ways."

As the oldest grandchild, Christy has seen her grandfather go out of his way many times to enjoy God's creation with his grandchildren—like making a landing on a lake or taking a special trip by boat to see a moose.

She remembers when her grandparents grew watermelons and cantaloupe at their camp near Pella. "He'd show us how to test it," said Christy. "When I was younger, I remember his demonstrating more and doing more, and teaching."

Combining corn and soybeans provided Gary another opportunity to connect. All the grandchildren have gone combining with him. "Do the grandkids want to come out and take a ride with me?" Gary would ask his children at harvest time. In 2006, Gary took Granddaughter Heidi and Great-grandson Xander combining with him.

One time, Mindi brought home friends from college who wanted to go combining, and they each did a couple rows with him. Mindi's husband Frank tried it, too.

Though Gary reached out through his activities and interests, he left the emotional connecting to Matilda. Conversing with Gary wasn't always easy—even for his own family members.

"He is not one to make happy talk. That is what I learned as I got to be more comfortable with the family," said Dale Andringa. "You have to know what interests him at a given point in time. We didn't discuss the weather. What's the point? The weather is what it is. Get him on a subject that he is interested in at that moment in time, and he can talk forever."

"He's very quiet. He has certain things that he's interested in, and if he's interested you have a good conversation," said Grandson Dan Vermeer. "Then, when you're done talking about it, the conversation is over. You can't really make small talk with him.

"I think he's from the old World War II generation mentality, being a man of few words," Dan added. "I remember times of quiet, and we would just enjoy the activity."

That has been Jason's experience, too. "My grandpa is never the type to ask you how your life is. He'll never ask those questions, and I've never minded," said Jason. "Some will say Grandpa is intimidating [because he didn't talk much]. That would never bother me. We would talk about airplanes or fishing, and a lot of times we wouldn't talk."

Mindi talked with Gary a lot about basketball, about her own games playing for Pella Christian High School and Calvin College, or about the teams from nearby Lynnville-Sully. "I would often ask him about farming or fishing, his early experiences."

"He's kind of abrupt. I don't think anyone feels super warm and fuzzy around him, but he treats everyone the same," said Heidi.

And like probably just about every man of his generation, Gary isn't what Granddaughter Heidi calls "the huggy type." She commented, "I give him a hug frequently. He's not a huggy type person, but I am, so I just give him a hug anyway. He doesn't totally know what to do with that."

Christy, displaying the kind of innocent mischievousness that her grandfather himself will show on rare occasions, confessed, laughing, "My cousin, Heidi, and

I like to hug him on purpose, and he doesn't really know what to do. It's kind of funny—we figure he's never too old to learn."

Gary and a Crowd

Though Gary may be reticent to be drawn into a living room conversation, put him on a stage in front of a crowd, and he is, as Jonathan described him, "dynamic and funny and very comfortable with public speaking."

Gary was a natural in front of a crowd.

Converse with Gary, and his frequent wry understatements are delivered so soberly that a lone listener is left wondering if he's serious or joking. Put Gary on stage, however, and his understated delivery can be downright hilarious and his timing, perfect. Although better heard live on stage, that humor also comes alive in print.

During his fiftieth wedding anniversary celebration, when he talked in front of a near-capacity crowd at the Pella Opera House—it holds 324 people—he spoke warmly of his courtship of Matilda with details that were startlingly intimate:

> I used to talk with the boys about the girls. I don't think they do that anymore but they did then. They told me that after you have a girl out for one or two nights, you ought to give her a good night kiss. That was a problem for me because I didn't know how to go about that. I had three brothers. I never kissed any of them.

He continued his story:

> So I thought for a whole week about this. How am I going to do this? I was also told that sometimes girls don't like it, and they slap you in the face. So I figured it all out: I'll take her by the arms. And I'll give her a quick kiss. I walked Matilda from the car to the house. I was about ready to do it when I lost my nerve. I just said good night and I went home.

When he spoke about his dad to production crews filming a video in honor of Vermeer Manufacturing Company's fiftieth anniversary in 1998, Gary remembered, "He thought if I didn't farm, I wouldn't make any money." After a half-second pause and with only a hint of a smile, Gary added, "He was wrong."

His way of talking is simple. He may have been the richest man in the room, but he was as common as anyone there, as demonstrated in his opening for a 1997 speech to an antique tractor club:

> Okay, I should be able to get along with you folks pretty good because I imagine some of you folks are farmers—maybe about all of you are farmers. And that's basically what I am, too. I never did quit farming. I am still a farmer. We have about 1,600 acres, and I plant all the corn, and I harvest all the corn and beans on the farm, so I guess I'll fit right in with you folks."[15]

Connecting With Grandchildren

Gary and Matilda's first grandchild, Christy, was born 6,000 miles away in Nigeria, where Margaret and Stan were living and teaching at the time. Gary and Matilda went on to have seven other grandchildren and, by 2008, nine great grandchildren, but never again did they live so far away from their progeny.

When Christy was almost three, her family returned to Iowa so that Margaret could seek cancer treatment from a family friend in Iowa City. Matilda was always willing to care for Christy and Jonathan during this time and also later after Margaret's death.

"After mom died, part of our routine was—if we weren't in school—we would go to Grandma's house a couple days a week," said Christy. "She'd always make your favorite foods, whether that was tater tot casserole or Lucky Charms for breakfast."

Christy said she often watched *The Sound of Music*. She suspects her brother Jonathan dislikes that movie because she watched it so much. *The Sound of Music* was one of two movies her grandparents owned. The other was *Fiddler on the Roof*, which the young Christy didn't understand and therefore didn't watch. Often the children played outside—feeding pigs, playing with kittens, and playing on hay bales.

Jonathan, Christy, and Mindi sit next to the hay bale while Heidi, Dan, and Jason sit on top.

At the end of the day, especially if he were farming, Gary came into the house and asked Christy to help him take off his work boots. "He'd sit in his chair, and he'd loosen the shoe laces. I'd tug and tug, and all of a sudden I'd go flying with the boot. He thought that was great fun."

Gary also taught his granddaughter to stand on her head. He showed her how to get down in a tripod—with her head and two hands on the ground and put her knees on her elbows. "He'd show me how to do it. I remember trying and trying in the living room."

Gary gives some of his family a ride at the Woody Place, 1984.

Later, when Mary started working part-time at Vermeer in January 1982, her son Jason was six and daughter Mindi was almost four. They frequently stayed with their grandparents during the workday and for longer periods when Mary and Dale traveled out of town for business.

When Mindi was young, she went to her grandparents two or three times a week, along with the family's beagle, Snickers, so-named because he looked like a candy bar. "My grandpa was a dog lover. He'd laugh at how funny our dog was," Mindi recalled. "One morning, I woke up, and they gave the dog a bowl of cereal because they didn't know what else to give him."

Mindi also remembers that her grandparents set up a basketball hoop at their house for her "and Grandpa would shoot with me. He'd take a shot or two, and he'd be done."

But the game she and all the other grandchildren best remember playing with their grandparents is cards. "When I was really little, he would play Go Fish or Old Maid," Allison remembered. As the grandchildren got older, they played Pitch, Rook, and Hearts—often. They played in their grandparents' home, and they played almost every night while in Canada. They even played cards while on a safari in Africa.

"Towards the later part of the evening, Grandpa would purposely try to 'shoot the moon' and would generally lose and say, 'Oh shucks, I have to go to bed now,'" said Mindi. She knew his bid to be exactly what it was: a ruse to go to bed.

Matilda also made sure the grandchildren stayed connected by inviting the families, one at a time—a manageable number for her kitchen table—to Sunday dinner after church.

When the family arrived, the scene was predictable. Matilda was busy in the kitchen. Gary was sitting in his chair reading *The Banner*, a periodical of the Christian Reformed Church.

"They are unique in how their lives spell out love to family," said Lois Vermeer. "For Gary it is activity: doing adventures. For Matilda it is food. Food is huge: cooking up the wild game, favorite desserts, Sunday dinners. Nothing pleases her more than her grandchildren and children finishing all the mashed potatoes."

The grandchildren loved their grandmother's meals. "Grandma cooked up an awesome meal. What she makes, she makes so good, and we'd be really ready to eat," said Heidi.

Dinners were usually traditional. Sometimes Matilda put a pot roast in the oven before leaving for church. David remembers a chicken and gravy dish she made by slow-cooking chicken hindquarters. She took the meat off the bones and mixed it into a thick hearty gravy. She served this over mashed potatoes with green beans or peas.

Usually she had a fruit pie, such as cherry, for dessert. Sometimes, she made Pink Fluff, a creamy dessert with a pretzel crust.

One food David associates most with Matilda is *snijboontjes*, a Dutch method of preparing green beans. He grew to like these so much that he learned from Matilda how to make them:

> Wash green beans, and snap off ends. Run fresh green beans through a French-style bean cutter. Place beans in bowl and sprinkle heavily with pickling salt or canning salt. Work the salt through the beans with your hands. If there isn't enough brine created to cover the beans, then add more salt. Pack the beans into quart jars, and cover with the lids. There is no need to pressurize the jars; the salt will cure the beans. After storing the jars for a couple months, soak and wash the beans well several times to remove salt. Boil and serve.

Matilda enjoyed cooking for her family nearly all of her life. But it is clear that to her, being with her family was the best part of these family gatherings.

Matilda enjoys time with Bob and her grandchildren David and Allison on a Canadian lake.

Canada was the place that Gary and Matilda especially connected with their grandchildren. Their camp in Pella also was a place the grandparents loved sharing. And there was a third location: Woody Place.

Dan and Heidi at the Woody Place

The Woody Place is a favorite spot for cookouts.

Named after a former owner, Dean Woody, the 350 acres is mostly timber, located ten or fifteen miles from Pella in Jasper County.

Like the camp, Gary initially bought the property for hunting, and indeed it remains prime hunting ground. But Gary also built walking paths through the property and named them after his grandchildren.

At least twenty-five years ago, he had street signs made for each of his grandchildren and in recent years had the deteriorating signs replaced. The girls are avenues: Christy Avenue, Heidi Avenue, Allison Avenue, and Mindi Avenue. The boys are streets: Dan Street, Jon Street, Jason Street, and David Street.

The property is bottom land and provides an excellent habitat for the herons, whose nests Gary enjoys watching in the spring before the trees leaf out.

Over the years, the Woody Place has been a great place for Gary and Matilda when they took their walks, and a wonderful place for the family to gather, as they did to celebrate Gary's eightieth birthday in 1998, roasting hotdogs and marshmallows over a campfire.

The Grandchildren Grow Up

As the grandchildren became teenagers, Gary and Matilda continued to remain an active part of their lives. Gary taught his grandsons to hunt, and both he and Matilda attended the grandchildren's school and sporting events. They went to Dan's baseball games, to Allison's horse shows, and to Mindi's basketball games. Mindi was frequently surprised by her grandparents at her games, even away-games in Chicago or Ohio. "When I was in college, they came to about five or six of my games each year. I would run out on the court, and they'd be there."

Even as the grandchildren grew into adults, Gary and Matilda continued to maintain close contact with them. How close? Well, how many young men date with their grandparents?

Playing cards with grandsons David (left) and Jonathan

When Dan was dating Tricia, who later became his wife, he took her over to his grandparents to play cards—usually Four-Point Pitch. His cousin, Jason, went one step further. He and his girlfriend joined his grandparents on a trip to Alaska.

The summer after graduating from college, Jason and his girlfriend, Carrie, flew with his grandparents in Gary's Bonanza plane as far north as Barrow, Alaska—one of the northernmost towns in the world. There, Jason proposed to Carrie during a walk along the Arctic Ocean.

"My grandparents were the first to know I was engaged," Jason said, and he finds nothing odd about that. "I feel really close to them; they were almost like parents to me."

And when the grandchildren were away, Gary and Matilda traveled to them. The couple visited Mindi in Grand Rapids one or two times a year. They arrived in Grand Rapids on a Saturday afternoon, played cards together and enjoyed church together the next day.

Shortly after Mindi's twins were born in 2007, Gary and Matilda visited but couldn't hold them because they were still in incubators. So they returned at the end of March to see the babies when they were nearly two months old. Mindi figures that Gary held Jakob for forty-five minutes. "He held my son, and he really enjoyed it. He said he couldn't believe how little he was." They took a photo of Gary holding Jakob, Matilda holding Madeline, and Mindi holding the dog in her lap.

For several years, Gary and Matilda visited California when grandsons Jonathan and Jason both lived there. "We flew to Catalina Island about seventy miles offshore and visited a restaurant there at the airport. We would have buffalo burgers," said Jonathan. They went to the botanical gardens once, and Jonathan took his grandparents to see plays. "He always loved the theater, especially musicals. We'd usually try to plan activities to keep everyone busy. Grandpa liked going to Palm Springs where there is a tram going up the side of the mountain. The engineering side of him was fascinated."

Seeing Extended Family

On Monday nights, Gary and Matilda have a standing date. They go to McDonald's where they meet with Gary's brother John H. and his wife, Effie, as well as brother Dutch's widow, Jeannette "Jay," and brother Harry's widow, Bernice. John and Gary's first cousin, Marsha Overbergen, and her husband Jim also join them.

"They are a wonderful family," said Marsha. "They are so good to me because Gary and John are the only family I have left, other than my children. I always wanted brothers and didn't have any, so they were my brothers. We get together every week, and really have a good time."

The tradition probably got its start seven or eight years ago with Harry and Bernice, who always ate at McDonald's on Monday nights. "Once, Effie and I were there at the same time, and they asked us to join them," recalled John H. "Then they said, 'Why don't you join us next week and ask Gary and Matilda to come, too?' And that is how it got started."

Gary and Matilda in 2004 at West Market Park with Dorothy, John, Edith, and Evelena

"Harry thought it would be a good way to keep up with his brothers," said his widow, Bernice. "And Jeannette appreciated it so much."

Likewise, Matilda makes sure she remains connected to her siblings with regular visits, phone calls, and frequent dinners out on Thursday nights. For years, she organized a Van Gorp picnic over Memorial Day at their camp near Pella. More recently, the extended Van Gorp family gets together in July for a picnic at a Pella park.

A Family Legacy

What is the legacy Gary and Matilda leave their family?

First and foremost, Gary and Matilda modeled for their children and grandchildren a love of God and a life of faith, a model that all their descendents have followed.

Granddaughter Heidi explained just how meaningful that has been. "My Christian faith and my relationship with Jesus Christ are central to my life," said Heidi. "Both Grandma and Grandpa passed that on to me as we attended church together, prayed together, and read the Bible together. I learned from them that everything we have belongs to God."

Secondly, they modeled a life that was both generous and marked with humility. "They are very good stewards and also very humble," said Granddaughter Mindi. "They didn't really have to tell me to be a good steward or to be humble; they led by example. They are both so good at giving to those in need."

Gary and Matilda also involved their family in a way that was both unusually strenuous and inclusive.

Growing up in that environment, the children perhaps didn't notice it as much as others drawn into the family. When Dale Andringa joined the family in 1971, he was immediately struck by how active the family was. "You didn't have to worry about getting bored, because everyone in the family was active. The guys never went off and did one thing. Men and women—all generations—did it together. If it was hiking in the woods, we all went. Fishing was certainly not a guy thing; it was a family thing. Granddaughters were expected to enjoy it as much as the grandsons, and they did."

The Vermeer Family, 1960

The importance of involving and connecting family continues in other ways, too, with the second and third generation. Stan, blessed with an excellent memory and an interest in writing is the unofficial family historian. His daughter, Christy, creates family scrapbooks, providing a lasting memory and an historical record of many of the family trips and special occasions. Grandson Jason's wife, Carrie, makes sure she takes her children regularly to see their great grandparents.

Gary and Matilda have turned their grandchildren into world travelers. Grandson Jonathan, who inherited his grandfather's adventurous spirit, loves high-adventure sports like kayaking and rock climbing. Grandson Jason shares Gary's passion for flying. Grandson Dan shares his passion for hunting and fishing.

Vermeer Corporation is also a significant legacy. All three children and quite a few grandchildren have worked there. As the company celebrates its sixtieth anniversary, the company is led by Bob and Mary, who share the role of Chief Executive Officer. Grandson Jason and granddaughter Allison are also employed there.

In Search of a Better Way
The Lives and Legacies of Gary and Matilda Vermeer
163

The Vermeer Family, late 1990s

But what about farming? After all, Gary started as a farmer, and though he founded a multi-million-dollar company, traveled the world, and has given away millions to worthy causes, he continued to plant corn. He has always been a farmer at heart—and Matilda, a farmwife at heart.

None of their children or grandchildren has taken up that farming lifestyle. Yet, it could be said that Gary's love of farming continues in the second and third generation when they celebrate their farming ancestry and demonstrate their love of the earth.

"He's a very brilliant man, and what he passed on to us are those qualities of innovativeness," said David, the youngest grandchild. "He never forgot his roots, never let his success take away what made him.

"He started as a farmer, but he went beyond that and gave us tools to do what we wanted. He gave us opportunities," David added. "I love the land. I still really do enjoy nature, but not as a farmer. A lot of us inherited his love for the land, but we're showing it in different ways."

Gary hauled corn in wagons long before combines made the job easier. Note the bang boards on the right side of the wagon.

5 Always a Farmer

Look! There's a blue heron! And there's a mother and five ducklings! Do you see them Gary?

~ Matilda Vermeer, during a drive in May 2007

As soon as Matilda pointed out the birds during a spring drive in 2007, Gary grabbed his binoculars for a better look. Eighty-eight years old and retired from hunting and farming, Gary—who has personally seen more wildlife than many people have seen even in photos or movies—still wanted to get a good look at the birds on his land.

"Is the corn up?" Matilda asked a little later in their drive. She answered her own question. "Yes! It's just coming out. See it, Gary?"

Again, he looked intensely at the fields, scanning for signs of green. Gary is a perennial outdoorsman.

Acquiring Land

Gary's dad gave him his first farm—the 120 acres of flat farm ground at Vermeer Road and Adams Avenue, just a couple miles outside of Pella.

"Dad bought the sixty acres north of here before he married," Gary said. "When I told him in 1940 that I wanted to get married, he first said he would give me a farm by Leighton. Then he decided to buy the Grandia farm [adjoining the sixty acres Gary's dad already owned]. Grandia had bought the farm after World War I for $636 per acre during boom times. He had it for sale for years for a total of $10,000."

Gary's dad bought it for that price. "That way I had 120 acres, and Dad thought we could work together. It had a couple of old barns on it. In 1940, we tore down one of the old barns and built a new one."

Grandpa Jacob Vermeer with his grandson Stan plowing for potatoes.

"We laid the foundation on New Year's Day in 1941, and the day before we got married, we built a hay track in the barn [to help move hay in from the wagon.] I remember it was thawing weather, and the water was running down in the creek."

The second farm that Gary acquired is south of what was his dad's farm—south of the farm on which the Pella Nursery now sits. Gary bought it in 1956, or "maybe a little earlier." It had been owned by his Uncle Art and Aunt Bertha. Gary was the executor of their estate and bought the farm at auction "Later when I gave stock to the children and grandchildren, I gave this farm to Stan," Gary added. "He was more interested in land."

Throughout the 1950s, the 1960s, and even later, Gary and his son, Bob, continued to buy farm ground.

He bought 120 acres from John Vande Noord, the property north of town that became his camp. He bought 150 acres from Andrew Boat—the first of several tracts of adjoining land that now roughly covers 400 acres.

One of those tracts was purchased from Harold Van Zante. Gary was eating lunch at the Dutch Buffet one day, when Harold came in. "I'm quitting farming. Want to buy my land?" he asked Gary.

"What do you want for it?"

"$1,000 per acre."

Gary didn't hesitate. "I decided right then to buy it."

It wasn't the only time Gary was approached to buy property. Nor the only time Gary made a quick buying decision. When the Rietveld farm, roughly 250 acres, was for sale, the estate asked for sealed bids. No one made an offer. "They were scared of it because it had been tiled around 1900, and the tiling was plugged," Gary recalled. A representative of the estate approached him and asked him what he thought the land was worth. Gary suspected what was coming. "I thought I'd better make it low so I said $400 per acre. He asked, 'Would you give that?' I said,

'Yes I would,' and he said, 'You've got it.'"

All in all, Gary and Bob have at least 2,000 acres of farmland, of which about 1,800 acres is river bottom ground.

Why did Gary keep buying land? "Oh, my dad liked to buy land," Gary said. "He was buying land before he was married."

Perhaps Matilda's answer to that question is more accurate: "A new farm meant a new challenge to him."

Even into the twenty-first century, Gary was buying property. He bought the Den Adel Farm at an auction, paying $330,000 for 140 acres.

The Farm, the Factory—Co-Dependents

Gary's farm experience taught him firsthand what equipment would be helpful to farmers. In that respect, farming and the factory always went together for Gary. And initially, farming was his mainstay, his reliable source of income; he didn't take any salary out of the company.

"I remember Gary used to say he had to keep farming to pay for the factory," said Marsha Overbergen, who in 1951 became the first full-time secretary at Vermeer. "They hardly took any money out. Everything they made went right back into it."

Gary's financial dependence on farming lessened dramatically as the factory became more successful. Yet that doesn't mean that Gary became less dependent on the farm.

It's not just a legend, but a true story, Matilda says, that when Gary faced a knotty problem at the factory, he would say, "I need to go to the farm." Gary found sitting on a tractor, undisturbed by other problems, a good place to think and solve manufacturing issues.

"When it came to planting and harvesting, that took a higher priority. In the company, there were no meetings at those times of the year. He wanted to be out there doing the planting and harvesting," said Bob. "That gave him great joy and energized him. Often in difficult times, he would go to the farm and to the camp. It didn't stress him the way the work at Vermeer Manufacturing Company did."

The opposite was true as well. Gary used the factory to support his farming. The factory, for example, added value to his bottom land.

His first two farms were high ground, ground that was out of danger of flooding. But Gary knew he could do something with bottom land, land close to the North Skunk and South Skunk rivers—parallel rivers that flow from the northwest to the southeast straddling much of the area's farm ground. Gary's bottom land was good fertile ground, but always in danger of flooding.

He knew tiling was the solution. But he did not want to use his father's process: plowing furrows for the tile with a team of mules dragging a plow. There had to be a better way. When Vermeer Manufacturing Company started manufacturing its line of trenchers, Gary put the machines to work on his own ground, too.

Gary dug trenches into which he laid parallel underground lateral pipes—about four inches in diameter and sixty feet apart. The tile is contoured so that the pipe drains water from thirty feet on each side. This runoff flows into a larger main line and then into a ditch or pit.

Tiling the ground also requires building dikes along the creeks to hold back the river water. In the old days, thirty teams of horses pulled scrapers to build a dike. When Gary bought his land, he often employed factory personnel who used a dragline to raise the height of the dikes, which are now at least six feet high. He remembers he paid $400 per acre for some of his bottomland, which was a good price at the time. Today the land, with improvements, is worth ten times as much.

"He would buy the poorest ground, and make it the best ground because he had the tools to make it work," recalled Larry Groenenboom, a longtime Vermeer employee whom Gary often called upon when he needed mechanical help around the farm.

When making drainage ditches, Gary surveyed the land to determine the appropriate slope. Using his own survey equipment, he did the work himself— another skill he says he "just picked up how to do."

In addition to the tile, Gary placed eleven pumps on his bottom land to pump the water out of the pits, over the dikes, and away from the fields. In wet weather, these pumps run most of the time, pumping out about 300 gallons of water per minute and during those times requiring constant attention. Gary's farm manager, Marv Bruxvoort, or later, Ward Van Dyke, often made several trips a day to check on the pumps—three-mile round trips on a four-wheeler.

When the pumps broke down, it was up to the farm manager to get them fixed. If he wasn't able to do it himself, he could always turn to the factory for help. That's the way it was with most of Gary's equipment. If he needed equipment changed, he was apt to walk into the factory and ask for a modification. If some of his farm machinery broke down requiring specialized work, Gary would tell his farm manager to call Larry Groenenboom.

A 35-year employee of Vermeer Corporation, Larry Groenenboom still considers himself a farm boy. Because he shares Gary's love of farm equipment, he has become a close friend. "We both like to tinker with things. He has a lot better head on his shoulders than I have, though," Larry said.

"He always wanted to try something different. He was always thinking, always thinking. He would change the machines to try something different. Sometimes his ideas would work. Sometimes they wouldn't.

"Gary always, always, had a tape measure with him. And he thought everyone else should too," Larry added. "That's why my pocket is worn here. If you didn't have a tape measure with you, something was wrong with you."

Coffee Time Tradition

Traditionally, Iowa farmers have enjoyed a coffee time. In addition to a hot meal at noon, farmers generally took time out from their work for a coffee time about 9 a.m. and again at 3 p.m.—usually coffee and a sandwich. "My mother brought the coffee out to the field sometimes," Gary said. "And a sandwich with that nice ham on it. Once in a while I drank a cup of coffee with Dad."

That was the way it was for Gary's parents. And Matilda remembers that the first fall after her marriage, she was helping Gary pick corn when Gary's mother, Anna, brought buns with pressed chicken to the field. "It was so delicious!"

However, that tradition soon ended after Gary and Matilda married, though neither can exactly remember how or when. Gary never stopped for a coffee time; he usually just took a sandwich with him to eat at noon.

The exception, though, was when Gary and Matilda hosted a big group of threshers working on their farms. Those times were different. "Boy, when you threshed you had those big coffee times. Ladies spent a lot of time at that," said Gary.

Choosing Farm Equipment

As indicated earlier, Gary hired a farm manager for many years to help manage and work his farms. Only for a few years after his marriage did he farm by himself or in cooperation with his brothers. But shortly after he started the factory in 1948, he needed help on the farm. The hired man, the first of whom was Harold Van Maanen, took on much of the farm work.

In 1957, Marv Bruxvoort took on the job as hired man until 1962 when he went into a farming partnership with Gary and Lou Van Wyk, another farmer. Lou and Marv each had a quarter of the partnership while Gary held the other half. Sometime later, Marv bought out Lou's share.

During the twenty years that Marv was in partnership with Gary—until about 1981—the two men raised livestock in addition to the crops. It was Marv's responsibility to care for them. They fed out and sold about 100 head of cattle each year, and another 400 to 500 head of hogs. The cattle sometimes were in a field near Gary's home, other years in fields closer to Marv's home. Both Marv and Gary had farrowing sheds at their homes. They raised their own oats and alfalfa for the livestock, about twenty acres each, and, before the invention of the Vermeer baler, square-baled both the hay and straw.

When purchasing farm equipment, Gary liked to do business close to home. His tractors were John Deere, until the local dealership closed and he switched to International Harvester. His combines were New Holland, which he traded every few years for a newer model.

Gary bought New Holland combines and looked forward to the harvest every fall.

Marv will never forget one particular piece of equipment—a brand new six-row cultivator. Marv was using the machine for the first time when Gary stopped by.

"What time are you going to turn the pigs and sows out?" Gary asked.

"About 3:30 or 4:00," Marv told him.

"Fine," Gary said. "I'll be back to take over then."

When Gary returned, Marv had just finished cultivating that field. So Gary took the cultivator to another field, while Marv started on his livestock chores. Later, as Marv worked on his chores near Gary's home, he did a double take when he saw a cultivator being hauled down the road and realized it was their own brand-new cultivator. Gary had damaged it somehow when he got it caught up in a ditch.

Matilda came out of the house, grinned, and said to Marv, "I bet you're glad that Gary did that. Gary can never figure out how those things happen."

When Marv and Gary ended their partnership and Marv became Gary's farm manager instead, they sold their livestock. From then on, the farming operation involved just corn and soybeans.

Gary and Stan

Over the years, Gary's active participation in the farms ebbed and flowed. The summers in Canada precluded his farming activities for much of the summer, though not completely. Gary usually didn't go fishing until mid-May and hoped to have all the planting done before that, but it didn't always work out that way.

"Life does not get better than this," Gary told Dave Heinen, his guest in Canada over Memorial Day weekend in 1995. "For the next week, I get to do the two things in life that I most enjoy. I'm fishing in Canada for three days, and when I get home, I get to plant beans."[1]

Marv retired in 2001, and Ward Van Dyke became farm manager until Gary retired and held his farm sale in the fall of 2006. Ward described his job as farm manager for those few years as the person who took care of all the details—the seed, chemicals, equipment, and so on—so that everything was ready to go when Gary was ready to get into the fields.

Though Ward saw Gary's involvement decrease even over his few years, Gary always enjoyed running the equipment. Gary often ran the field cultivator, and Ward planted and sprayed. Even in his late eighties, Gary loved to combine, though if it became too dusty, Ward took over. He also loved to haul grain into town in the winter time, pulling a wagon with his tractor while Ward drove the semi. As recently as the fall of 2006, Gary combined most of the corn and beans, according to Ward. "He really enjoyed it. That's what he grew up with. He was a farmer from the beginning. Even this spring [in 2007], he field cultivated for me."

Back to the Good-Old-Ways

In the 1980s, Gary had the idea that it might be more economical for a farmer to buy a tractor-mounted corn harvesting system than to buy a combine. About that time Gary bought a Woods Brothers Corn Picker, very similar to the one-row picker Larry Groenenboom's dad had when he was growing up.

"Gary wanted to see how it worked because it was simple, and he thought he could make one like that," Larry recalled. Instead, that purchase started a decade-long tradition.

Each fall, Gary asked Larry: "Do you want to pick corn this year?"

And they would, with the old-fashioned corn-picker.

Gary would save twelve quarter-mile rows for harvesting the old-fashioned way. Larry had a 1936 B John Deere; Gary had a 1926 D.

Larry Groenenboom and Gary used a one-row corn picker to harvest a few rows for many years.

"So we would pick, sometimes with his D and the Woods Brothers picker. The D worked pretty good, but the crop was almost too good for the old picker. Gary's tractor didn't have a slow enough gear. So we thought, let's try my little B John Deere. It worked perfect! We would take the sideboards off the wagon and pull it behind the picker."

Because the one-row picker didn't shell the corn, the men transferred the corn back into the combine to shell it.

Later, Gary bought an old flare box wagon. It wasn't in the best of shape, so he had it rebuilt at the factory. He wanted an end gate like the old days. "So we got plywood and had it swing out, just like it used to be. I would have made it different, but we made it his way," Larry recalled.

Then they ran it through the factory's paint line. They also attached a cable hoist to it, just like the one Gary designed in the 1940s. "As years went on, we would pick in that old wagon."

For a decade, Larry and Gary used that wagon and the old corn picker to pick twelve rows of corn.

"Gary always called that wagon a sixty-bushel wagon. We would pick all morning for 300 bushels of corn. Five loads. We picked a long time for 300 bushels. That's nothing in this day and age. It was fun, but it was a lot of work. At night, I was tired. This way of doing things you don't do any more."

The man who said, "There ought to be a better way" had gone back to the old way.

Gary and Jason, 2½ years, on the Model D tractor

Before Gary's farm sale in December 2006, Larry asked Gary what he was going to do with the corn picker. Gary answered him, "I think I will give it to Larry Groenenboom."

Later, the farm auctioneer, Ray Veenstra, talked to Larry. "He didn't know I had the corn picker," recalled Larry. "He wanted to make a story of this at the auction: the corn picker is the way Gary started and the combine is how he ended."

Larry remembered, smiling, "The auctioneer's plan did not work out!"

Gary with his cross bow, 2005

6 Gary, Hunter and Pilot

One evening many years ago, we decided to go frog hunting at the camp. Gary, Art Rus, and I took our kids and some other people and went around the lake in boats. We shot a bunch of frogs and then went back to the camp and started cleaning them. Our wives fried them and served them up as the main course in a wonderful dinner. It made for a wonderful time to remember for all.[1]

~ John H. Vermeer, Gary's brother, 1998

At eight or ten years of age, Gary started hunting when his dad bought him an air rifle. He went over to the barn next to the silo. "I sat there for hours and shot at pigeons. Once in a while I would get one."

His four grandsons were about the same age when Gary introduced them to the sport that had become a passion over the years. When they were eight years old, he bought them a BB gun. When they turned twelve, he bought them an "over and under," a gun with a .22 rifle barrel on top and a .410 shotgun barrel on the bottom.

Gary hunted all kinds of game, including moose such as this one shot in Canada in 1962.

As teenagers, Jason and David showed only minimal interest in hunting, and Jonathan enjoyed the sport as a hobby. But Gary's oldest grandson, Dan, came to share his grandfather's pleasure in the sport, a passion he credits entirely to his grandfather. "I know I wouldn't have developed that if he hadn't been a hunter."

On one of his first hunts, Dan shot a squirrel with a shotgun. "You got it. Good job," was all that Gary told him. He never even mentioned that his grandson "blew it to bits," as Dan described it.

"In some ways, he was a very good teacher. He would give you the freedom to do it your own way."

Daily Duck Hunts

While in high school, Dan met his grandparents at 6 a.m. every day before school at Gary's duck blind a few miles north of town at the camp. Nearly buried in the dike along the water, the blind is as much a breakfast place for duck hunters as it is a camouflaged hideout from the ducks. From the entrance, hunters walk down a few steps into a kitchen and eating area. Here, Gary has hosted hundreds of breakfasts in the simple, but functional area. A camp stove, running water, a space heater, and a table and chairs provide everything hunters need. The blind's cement floor and metal walls keep the area dry. On the far side, a small door leads to a concealed outdoor area from which the hunters shoot.

On these early mornings before school, Dan and Gary often met family friends Marv and Carol Rus. Cousin Jonathan joined them on Saturdays. But Dan was steadfast; ready to hunt without fail every day except Sunday. He wore coveralls over his school clothes.

"Duck hunting was one of the things that motivated me to get my driver's license," Dan said. When he turned sixteen in July of 1986, he procrastinated getting his license. It wasn't until his mother told him she would no longer drive him out to the duck blind on those early fall mornings, that Dan finally got that license. He wasn't about to miss duck season with his grandfather!

Duck hunters usually start their morning scoping out the two lakes on the property to locate the ducks. If the ducks are at the larger lake, they shoot from the blind or hide themselves in the tall pampas grass nearby.

More often, the ducks are at an east-side, second lake where food is more plentiful. In the summer, Gary usually drains or lets this fifteen-acre lake go dry to allow grass to grow before he mows it and pumps water into it in the fall. "The ducks just love that—all that seed and grass," Gary said. "We shot 460 ducks there one year."

Once the hunters start shooting, the startled ducks fly off and usually are gone the rest of the day. So the duck hunting generally happens only in one place once a day, in the early morning. On Dan's hunts in high school, Marv Rus retrieved the ducks—wearing hip boots to wade in the smaller east lake and using a boat on the west lake.

After the shoot, the hunters headed back to the blind for breakfast. Dan remembers that Gary usually fried the eggs, while Matilda cooked the bacon.

The Vermeers always hoped their guests would take the ducks home. "When Marv shoots ducks, he has relatives who will take them. That's important. We are always happy if we don't have to take any home," said Gary.

"We give away as many of them as possible. We don't like them too well for eating," said Matilda.

Many local hunters consider themselves lucky to have been invited by Gary into the blind over the years. Kevin Van Wyk, a hunter who sometimes piloted Gary's plane to Canada, won't ever forget a hunt in 1989.

He recalled, "We were hunting ducks and geese together early one morning with Marv and Carol Rus. The morning was one of those where it was tough to see what was on the water."

The conversation soon turned to how hard it was for hunters to clearly see their targets in the early morning, so that they don't shoot a duck or goose out of season illegally. Kevin continued:

> Over breakfast, we started talking about another morning, when Art Rus [Marv's uncle and Gary's friend] had a similar problem. He actually shot ducks when he thought he was shooting geese. The rest of the hunting party apparently wouldn't let him forget his mistake, and in an effort to help him not make the same mistake, they prepared a booklet with pictures and diagrams. When the booklet was talked about, Marv thought that it was still in the cupboard somewhere, and he went looking for it and found it.

Gary started reading it and remembering his friend, Art. When he started reading, "Ducks go quack, quack, and geese go honk, honk," we all started laughing. I remember seeing Gary laugh so hard that he had tears in his eyes. This was special—I hadn't ever seen him laugh like that before.[2]

Squirrel Makes the Best Eating

Although Gary and Matilda did not enjoy eating duck, they thought squirrels—Gary calls them "bushy tails"—were delicious.

Gary liked to hunt squirrel particularly on the Rietveld place (Gary and Matilda refer to their properties by the former owners' names)—about five or ten miles north of town. The property is mostly open, mowed during the summers, with a few oak trees that attract squirrels.

Dan preferred squirrel hunting on his grandfather's property near the duck blind or over near his cousin Jonathan's home where it was more wooded. "Squirrel hunting was the hunting I did the most. You usually got something.

"A typical Saturday for my cousin Jon and me was that I would pick Jon up, and we'd go duck hunting early in the morning and then squirrel hunting the rest of the morning. We'd clean the squirrels over at Grandma's—and she'd probably give us some lunch."

Gary was usually there for the duck hunts, and occasionally, he'd be in on the squirrel hunts, too. One year, the three of them bagged seventy-five squirrels in the season, which runs from September 1 through the end of the year. "One year, Grandpa by himself shot sixty squirrels," said Dan.

To hunt squirrel, a rifle is best. Shooting one with a BB gun or a shotgun scatters fur all over the meat. "The last couple of squirrels, Gary used a .410, and I had to fish out all the hairs where the pellets were," Matilda said.

After their hunts, Dan and Jonathan cleaned the squirrels together—taking five to ten minutes for each one. "Grandpa could probably whip through one even faster than that," Dan said.

The Vermeers weren't people to let the meat go to waste. "Grandpa and Grandma ate a lot of them," Dan said. They often gave the meat away, too.

Today, Dan isn't so keen on squirrel meat anymore, which he describes as tasting like dark chicken meat. "You look at a squirrel, and it looks like something you wouldn't want to eat. You have to slow cook them. Grandma would cook them, and make them taste really good."

Squirrel meat often found its way to the Sunday dinner table Matilda spread out for her family after church—squirrel, along with chicken, mashed potatoes, and green beans. As a preschooler, Granddaughter Allison was confused by the cleaned meat when she peered at her first-ever platter of squirrel. She asked, puzzled, "Where's the fuzz?"

And as the oldest grandson, Dan always chose squirrel when presented a choice at the Sunday dinners. "I always thought you were a wimp if you ate the chicken."

Hunting Deer: Bow Season

For thirty years, Gary has joined a group of deer hunters who meet every Saturday at Gary's camp during bow season, which runs through October and November.

Men such as Jim Emmert, Mat Keske, Ben Van Zee, Ivan Brand, Paul Vander Hart, and Don Van Maanen have been part of the group over the years.[3]

Each year, the bow hunters make sure the deer stands are in working order for the season. In September, a group of men check the stands that Gary had custom-made at the factory. The metal part of the structure is left in the trees year-round, but the floor boards, stored during the off season, need to be put back in and the entire structure checked for safety.

Jim Emmert, one of the regulars, recalls that Gary used to come out to help with that work in September. "He came out to help us, and said 'I can't be of much help.' But he showed up with an end loader [to lift the workers up to the stands] which cuts our work by probably seventy-five percent!"

Each Saturday during the season, the hunters meet at Gary's camp at 6 a.m. for

The bow hunters target practiced at Gary's camp before they went out to hunt.

breakfast, always bacon, eggs, and toast. Gary hardly ever eats breakfast with the hunters—though in the early years he stopped in to say hello and grab a piece of bacon, then joined the duck or goose hunters already at the duck blind, before returning for the deer hunt.

After breakfast, the bow hunters practice their shots for a few minutes on a target Gary attached to a round bale near the cabin. Then they head out for the hunt—to the first of three or four locations they will hunt that day. Most are on Gary's land.

Jonathan and Heidi liked to climb their grandfather's deer stands.

Once at their hunting site, the group splits. Half climb the deer stands. The other half spread out and chase deer toward the waiting hunters. Then they switch. They generally make two passes through a property.

"Grandpa was outstanding with a bow," said Dan. "At twenty yards, all his arrows would be in an area the size of your fist."

"Gary called up a company and had them custom-build a scope to put on his compound bow." said Jim Emmert, a fellow hunter for the past thirty years. "He was pretty accurate with that thing. If he shot, he usually got one."

Later, approaching eighty, Gary enlisted the help of his physician to prove to the state of Iowa that he had a sufficient handicap to obtain state approval to use a crossbow. A crossbow takes significantly less arm strength to shoot than a compound bow, and also is significantly more powerful.

Over the years, Gary has shot thirteen deer with a bow. "You see them coming, and you pull the bow back," Gary said. "I had a couple of days I shot two of them in one day."

Though Gary stopped actively hunting a few years ago, he still likes to watch the hunt from his vehicle parked in the woods. He still wants to know how many deer are on the property.

Three times over the past thirty years, Jim recalls the group worrying about Gary. Gary, whose heart sometimes raced, would have to sit down and rest until his heart slowed. Then he would go home alone. "He's a stubborn Dutchman. No one's going to ride with him," said Jim, who, as a trained paramedic, would gladly have accompanied him. After fifteen minutes or so, the hunters would call Matilda to make sure that Gary got home okay.

The group could get one deer per deer license. They field dressed them and took pictures before they hauled them back in a pickup. Thirty years ago, they put the deer in a freezer at Pella Nursery and butchered them all at once. More recently, they're just as likely to butcher them in someone's garage. Gary supplies a big meat grinder for the job.

In the early days, Matilda and some of the other wives often participated. "I once walked in a circle and got lost—I saw the same tree over again!" said Matilda. "Later someone told me the same thing happened to her, and I felt better about it."

Hunting Deer: Shotgun Season

In Iowa, there are two short shotgun seasons for deer. The first begins the first Saturday in December and runs through the following Wednesday. The second starts the second Saturday in December and lasts a week.[4]

The logistics of these hunts with Gary are similar to the hunts during bow season. Everything is done in an extremely safe and well-organized manner.

A week or two before the season opens, group leaders talk about where they want to hunt and how they can improve upon the hunts of the previous years. Early on the first day of the hunt, the hunters gather at 5:30 or 6:00 a.m. at Gary's cabin and start with eggs, bacon, toast, jelly, and what they affectionately call "road tar," homemade sorghum syrup—a dark, sweet, and thick spread locally made by Maasdam Sorghum Mills in nearby Lynnville. After breakfast, they head out to the first of several properties they hunt that day.

At the hunting ground, half the group position themselves strategically, perhaps in the deer stands, while the others flush the deer out.

In bow season, Gary's hunting group numbers ten or fewer. They walk quietly because they don't want the deer on the run—bow hunters need a deer to be close and still in order to kill it.

In shotgun season, however, the hunters are more numerous, so it is less likely for the deer to slip through the cracks of their advance. They also yell a bit to let others know where they are and to get the deer moving.

When Gary hunted, he often went with a group of hunters. The hunts were always well organized.

The hunters are usually successful—sometimes bagging as many as four in a morning. "I always try to get them through the lungs." Gary grinned. "If I shoot the tail off I don't get them."

Ward Van Dyke remembers one year when they "tagged out," that is, they shot all the deer they legally could on the first Saturday morning. (Because all hunters each get one tag, the group can shoot

In Search of a Better Way
The Lives and Legacies of Gary and Matilda Vermeer
189

only as many deer as there are tags.) Tagging out early was a disappointment because it meant they were done for the season. After that year, they were careful to remind each other to wait for the big deer. And there were always plenty of them. "The most we ever had was thirty deer," said Ward.

Hunting is a time the men always looked forward to. "It's the experience of it all," said Ward. "There are a lot of laughs, carrying on, and story telling. The thrill of seeing the deer and all the other wildlife—it's awesome." For Ward, who hunted at first with his dad and now with his own sons, the tradition is also important, as are the organization and safety of the hunts.

After the kill, the hunters field dress the deer, (removing the intestines and vital organs), then throw the carcasses into the pickup to haul to Ward's machine shed. Later they haul them to the shop of Wayne Van Dyke (Ward's dad). There they make use of a couple chain hoists to hang the carcasses while they butcher.

Generally, butchering is on Wednesday afternoon, and everyone who showed up for the hunts is expected to show up for this work, too. And, like the hunts themselves, the butchering is organized to a T. "Everybody has a job to do," says Ward. Some do the skinning, others boning, others grind the meat making use of the grinder that Gary has bought and lends specifically for this purpose. In about four hours, the work is done. Some men take a section home with them, such as a loin. Some meat is ground. Ward likes to take some meat home with him to make jerky that he chews on during the following year's hunt. The bulk of it, however, goes to IntVeldt's, a local meat shop that will turn the meat into bologna—a venison version of a local delicacy known as Pella Bologna, a flavorful, smoky meat, generally made in a ring.

The venison bologna, like all the meat, is distributed equally among the hunters.

Circling Around the Fox

Over the years, Gary hunted fox with two different groups of hunters. One group, apparently organized by Harold Van Zee and John Gosselink, got together at 10 a.m. on Tuesdays for the hunt. At the start of the hunt, the hunters arranged themselves as if around a perimeter—a quarter- to a half-mile square—and then walked toward the center.

For years, Gary joined a group of hunters to hunt fox.

"We shot a lot of foxes out west of Pella," Gary said. "By the coal mines once they shot fifty times—at one fox! But he stayed just out of range." Gary figures this group got started when he was in his twenties and probably lasted for about fifteen years. The hunters skinned the foxes and sold the pelts to Harold Van Zee, who was a fur buyer. Gary says as many as sixty hunters might have shown up. Other times it was only ten to fifteen.

Later, Gary went fox hunting with a group from the factory, recalled Keith Nibbelink, a forty-two-year employee who started at the factory in 1954. These hunts were on Saturdays, but worked the same way: the hunters gathered around the outside edge of an area and then walked toward the center.

There was a bounty on the foxes, Keith remembered, so the hunters took a piece like the lower lip or the ear to the county and got paid for each one they had shot.

Foxes were a nuisance at the time, and would kill chickens. Farmers, especially, were glad to be rid of them.

Shooting With the Camera

After the official hunting seasons were over, Gary often wasn't ready to give up the hunt. So he hunted with his camera. "It would be very much like deer hunting except with cameras," said Dan.

Gary piloted a plane and later his helicopter, using them to drive the deer. Though Dan's memory is vague, he remembers going once when it was very cold. He had a cheap camera and was disappointed when the deer didn't show on the photos.

"Today in Iowa, you see deer all the time," said Dan. "That's not how it used to be. If you saw a deer when you were driving, that would be like 'whoa!' That would be news you'd tell people."

Al Van Dyke, a retired ag territory manager for Vermeer, recalls when Gary stopped at the plant on Saturdays and asked those working if they wanted a ride in his plane. Of course, the men said yes. After Gary landed the plane with his passengers, the men drove the deer toward Gary so that he could take pictures.

Gary also used a camcorder to record action photos of wildlife. More recently, he used a motion-sensitive camera at night that took flash photos.

The Hunting Grounds

As indicated in a previous chapter, one favorite hunting place is a piece of property in nearby Jasper County—roughly 350 acres in all—called the Woody

Place. Gary bought it specifically for hunting, though over the years it also became a favorite place for walks and family gatherings.

Jim Emmert remembers when one of the favorite hunting areas was owned by a farmer who permitted people to cut firewood for $5 a pickup load. It was not unusual for the hunters to be up in a tree stand and hear chain saws in the distance. How that piece of property became owned by Gary is now one of the many legends circulating about him:

"The story has it that Gary was flying his plane over this hunting area and noticed that several trees had been cut down for firewood. Apparently this didn't settle well with Gary, and he returned to the air-strip, got in his car, and drove to the farmer's house. Gary asked him 'If you were going to sell this land today, how much would you ask?' The farmer shot Gary a price, and Gary took out his check book and wrote the farmer a check for that amount. That is how Gary came to own one of our hunting areas."

Flying for Pleasure

Gary gave many family members, friends, and employees rides on his plane. Pictured here are Matilda, Mary, Anna (Gary's mother), Bernice, and her four children.

That an Iowa farmer like Gary hunted isn't surprising— though the magnitude of the organization behind the hunts is remarkable. However, Gary's other hobby, flying, is more unusual. And like his hunting, he embraced this hobby wholeheartedly.

"As soon as he had his license in 1950, in March, we had to go up, and I had to go along," Matilda recalled. Mary, born the previous November, was just a few months old. "I said, 'We can't take such a small baby up!' But I asked the doctor, and he said it was okay. I had nervous legs the first time we went up with Gary!"

Gary soon bought his first plane, a Piper Clipper—a twenty-foot plane with a wingspan of just over twenty-nine feet that could seat four people tightly. In 1949, a Piper Clipper sold for $2,995.[5]

"Mary has always loved flying and has never gotten sick or anything," recalled Matilda. "We flew once to California in the summer. It was so bumpy. Stan and I felt sick. Mary said, 'Oh this is fun!' I asked Gary, 'Why in the world did we go when you knew how bumpy it would be?'"

After the Piper Clipper, Gary bought a single-engine Bonanza, the first of a series. It was the Bonanza that Gary used while vacationing with his family and to ferry so many people to Canada. First introduced in 1947, the Bonanza was a popular plane built by the Beech Aircraft Corporation. It distinguished itself among other aircraft by sporting a V-shaped tail to reduce drag and weight. By the end of 1947, Beech Aircraft's plant in Wichita, Kansas, had delivered 1,000 of these planes, which sold initially for $7,975.[6]

Gary really liked flying the Bonanza. "It could carry four people easily, and it could fit five when the kids were small. We have had seventeen of those. We would buy one, fly 1,000 hours, and trade it off. You could do it for $20,000 in those days."

Over the years, Gary owned two twin-engine Cessnas. Because they have two engines, they are considered to be a little safer. In addition, Gary owned two Cessna 185s at different times that he turned into the floatplanes he used for so many years at the Canadian border. He sold his last floatplane in 2006.

Besides their speed and convenience, Gary found his planes to have other advantages. "Driving a plane is a lot easier. You don't have to worry about the other cars."

Gary initially obtained a regular pilot's license, but by the time he quit piloting, he held single engine, multi-engine, helicopter, seaplane, and instrument ratings.

Gary's initial partners in the business, Brother Harry and Cousin Ralph, both obtained pilot's licenses, which they used extensively for both business and pleasure. And, as mentioned earlier, quite a few others at the factory also obtained their licenses at Gary's urging. All three of his children got their licenses—Stan flew extensively for Vermeer when he was employed there and also piloted the floatplane for more than a decade in Canada. Even Matilda took flying lessons for a time when she was fifty years old, mostly so she could land the plane if Gary had a heart attack or some other sudden health problem in the air.

All three children have let their licenses lapse; however, Grandson Jason inherited his grandfather's passion. Jason started taking flying lessons at the Pella airport when he was fifteen. At sixteen, he soloed, and at seventeen, he got his license. The following winter, he obtained his instrument rating. In 2000, Jason obtained his multi-engine and commercial rating so that he could fly Vermeer's first jet.

Now Vermeer Corporation has a Beechcraft Premier I jet that will carry eight people, including two pilots, and also a Cirrus SR22, a small prop plane that

Gary fuels his floatplane before heading out to a remote Canadian lake.

carries four people, including the pilot, for shorter hauls. Jason holds a type rating and has flown enough hours that he can fly the jet as "pilot in command," and is certified but not yet insured to fly the jet single-pilot.

Jason developed his love for flying during the trips to Canada with his grandfather.

"My first summer [flying to Canada] he was still clearly better than I was," Jason said. So when storms threatened, Gary took over the controls. But it wasn't very long before Jason took over the controls in bad weather. And for six weeks over each of five summers—from 1993 to 1997—Jason served as Gary's bush pilot in Canada.

To Alaska, Twice

Two of the family's most memorable flying experiences were probably their trips over the mountains to Alaska. The first, in 1960 when he was yet in his early forties, Gary piloted Matilda and their three children in the Bonanza.

The couple returned to Alaska in 1999, this time with Grandson Jason at the controls of a single-engine Bonanza A36 and accompanied by Carrie Anderson, who, as indicated in chapter 4, became Jason's fiancé during the trip.

It wasn't just the engagement that made the trip so memorable for Jason.

"Wow! Flying from Grande Prairie [Alberta] to Fairbanks [Alaska] was undoubtedly the highlight of my flying experiences," Jason wrote in his journal in August 1999. "Flying in the mountains is beautiful. I feel like I'm flying with nature but apart from it, above it."

At one point on the trip, they flew near "gigantic snow-covered peaks, one up to 17,260 feet. We flew over blue glacial lakes and brown glacial braided rivers, some hundreds of feet wide. I could see glaciers nestled into the mountains."

Matilda's experience flying over Alaska's Brooks Range, however, was tinged with worry. "I didn't feel very good," she recalled in 2007 as she reminisced about the trip. "I said, 'You always need to be looking for a place to land. Where would you land here?' Jason said, 'Oh, I would find a place.'"

"That was an interesting trip, though," Gary added. "After that range, the land slopes down all the way to the Arctic Ocean. We landed at Denali Park; the runway wasn't very long there. We stepped it off. But we had no trouble getting off."

Jason wrote about that landing in his journal: "The landing was very tight between mountains on all sides. The strip was gravel, 3,000 feet long. Very exciting landing and airport to be at."

On the return trip, Jason started picking up ice on the plane. "We made it from McKinley to Whitehorse [Yukon] today, but couldn't get any farther due to the weather," he wrote on August 8, 1999. "I was picking up ice on my wings and windshield at 11,000 feet…. That is the first time I have ever had ice. It definitely slowed our air speed."

On that trip, Jason handled the controls except for the last leg when Gary, then nearly eighty-one years old, took over and flew the plane from Fargo, North Dakota, back home to Pella.

A Lifetime Passion

For his first fifteen or twenty years of flying, Gary kept his planes at the Pella airport. In 1967, he built a landing strip at Vermeer Manufacturing Company, and for a time stored his planes in four hangars at the plant. The planes today are at the Pella airport.

As much as Gary flew, he always made sure he knew the limits and capabilities of his plane and the requirements he needed for a runway.

Longtime employee Marv Vander Werff recalled watching Gary in action in Storm Lake, Iowa. Vermeer Manufacturing Company was trying to dig across the ice on Storm Lake so that a phone company could throw a cable into the lake, a process they thought would be more efficient than digging around the lake's perimeter. "Gary wanted to see this work, so Gary and I flew up there together," said Marv. "It was cold—we had a [Vermeer] machine on the ice, so you know the ice had to be thick. When we landed at the Storm Lake airport, we landed clear to one side of the runway, not in the center. I thought that was strange, but I didn't question Gary Vermeer!

"When we were leaving, we taxied to the end of the runway. Gary stopped the plane and asked me to get out and step off half of the runway [width]. I don't remember how many steps it was. Later, when I heard people talking about how narrow the Vermeer runway was, I realized what had happened. That was how Gary determined the width of the Vermeer runway. He tested it in Storm Lake to see if he could land on half. He could, and then asked me to step it off to learn how wide that was."

In the mid-seventies, Gary bought the first of two helicopters, and several people remember fondly their first rides. Vince Newendorp, who as a youth lived near Gary's brother Dutch, got his first helicopter ride when Gary was giving rides from Dutch's house one day. Gary's former farm manager, Marv Bruxvoort, and his wife, Betty, won't ever forget flying with Gary in the helicopter to Des Moines for dinner. Primarily, though, Gary used the helicopter to check on the dikes and the pumps that held back floodwater from his farmland. He flew to each pump, landed, greased and then started the pump, then flew on to the next one. Vermeer construction crews had made cement pads near some of the pumps that Gary used as landing platforms.

All in all, he owned a helicopter for less than ten years, and logged maybe 1,000 hours at the most. "He didn't go long distances with the helicopter," said Matilda. He was, as she put it, "a boy with a big toy."

In 1994, Gary gave up his medical certificate, which meant he could no longer sit in the left seat or be a solo pilot. "I thought I was going to quit at seventy, but I kept going until I was seventy-six."

But Gary didn't really quit. Though he didn't have his medical certificate, he continued flying, albeit alongside another licensed pilot, for years after. He has logged more than 12,000 hours of flight time over fifty years of flying—for business and for the pleasure of his family, employees, and friends.

The pristine Canadian lakes always had a trophy fish.

7 Four Decades of Canada Fishing

The fishing in Canada was great, and eating the fresh-caught fish on shore, fried over an open fire was simply mouthwatering. Gary, you have given so many people interesting times in their lives, and I thank you for what you have given me.[1]

~ Keith Nibbelink

They say that some things can't be described. They can only be experienced.

That probably is true for the hundreds of people who were fortunate enough to go on a three-day fishing trip to Canada with Gary Vermeer.

Who can describe what it's like to gaze out the window of a small floatplane over the seemingly endless Canadian wilderness—admiring pristine lakes and an occasional waterfall—when suddenly Gary yells, 'There's one!' and dives so you can catch your first glimpse of a moose?

Who can describe the forlorn sound of the loons over the water? The woodsy smell of the air? The fried taste of the walleye you caught an hour earlier? The startled look of a moose with her calf?

And who can express what it's like to be treated with complete and humble hospitality by a couple who have given away more money than most could earn in a lifetime? Or what it's like seeing the personal side of a man who in every other setting seems so overwhelmingly serious?

Attempting the Impossible

Describing what it's like may just be impossible.

But still we try.

> We had never done anything like that before. It was so special to us that Gary was so kind to take us for the airplane ride and fishing. . . . That trip is something we will never, never forget.[2]
>
> > *The Bob Taylor family who happened to be vacationing in Canada in 1975 at the same time as the Vermeers and were invited for a plane ride*
>
> [Those] three days [were] the greatest fishing and hiking I have ever done. We fished from the boat and from a raft. Gary cooked the lunch, and we ate on the lakeshore. Gary is a true outdoorsman. . . . I will cherish these memories the rest of my life.
>
> > *Henry Black (an employee) of a July 1976 trip*
>
> I had been at Vermeer for two years and was given the gift of going on a fishing trip. . . . What an honor. . . . This was a first for me on many things.

. . . It was the first time for flying on a small plane and then a pontoon boat. I had never gone out on a lake and fished from a boat. The fish I caught was the biggest I have ever caught. This was an awesome experience.

> *Stanley Heersink (an employee) of his 1982 trip*

The first afternoon we went fishing at Lake Wesley. We took fifteen northern and nineteen walleye back to the camp. We fried some of them up for supper, which was delicious. The second day we went fishing on Sharp Lake. We had a delicious shore lunch of fresh fried fish, pork and beans, bread, and homemade oatmeal raisin cookies.

> *Carol Ver Woert (an employee) of a July 1985 trip*

We remember the quietness like we have never experienced before as we sat in the boat fishing or on the shore eating our noon lunch listening to the call of the loon.

> *Vern and Harriet Haagsma and their son Greg (fellow members of Faith Church) of their July 1992 trip*

For a man who avoided small talk and absolutely hated gossip, a man most comfortable alone in his tractor seat, a man who sought out nature and not cities, Gary was amazingly social at times.

Hundreds of people flew to Canada with Gary, and many times were joined by Matilda as well. These included close friends and mere acquaintances. These included employees from the plant who won a trip, widows who never experienced anything like that before, people who had never been fishing, people who loved fishing, people who had never been in a plane, people with whom he had hunted, people from the church, people from the community, people who farmed.

For weeks every summer spanning close to forty years of his life, Gary entertained family, friends and near strangers on three-day excursions to the Canadian wilderness.

"Gary and Matilda would bring up lots of people," said Jerry Lundy, who ran the camp for fourteen of the years the Vermeers visited. "They would seek out people who were down on their luck, maybe lost a loved one, and bring them up. And everything was free."

Brenda and Rick Gritters, May 1998

Gary's son-in-law, Dale Andringa, was often amazed at the people Gary and Matilda invited. "They frequently invited people who had never been there before," Dale said. "They provided people who would not have had the opportunity with that chance.

"I still have people tell me their trip with Gary and Matilda was one of the highlights of their life," Dale added.

The logistics of the trips were similar. The group started early, generally leaving Pella by 7 a.m. on Gary's Bonanza, a single-engine plane that could seat four people including the pilot. Especially in his younger years, Gary himself piloted the plane. Other times, his grandson Jason, Kevin Van Wyk, Rick Gritters, Jim Doezel, Stan Vermeer, or others hired by Gary piloted the plane.

In Search of a Better Way
The Lives and Legacies of Gary and Matilda Vermeer
205

Gary filleted the fish at the lake before taking them to camp. Here Gary is filleting fish on a homemade table on the plane floats at Lake Matilda.

From Pella, they flew to the Baudette International Airport, an airport much smaller than the name implies. The airport is right on Minnesota's border with Canada. Airport personnel drove them to their floatplane on the river; they taxied the floatplane across Rainy River to Canada to go through customs before flying off to their cabin.

By noon, they were at their camp. By 1 or 2 p.m., they had their first walleyes on their lines.

Moose First Lure Gary to Canada for Hunting

Ontario is Canada's most populous province. Well more than three-quarters of its population live in its cities, chiefly on its east side. More than four million people alone live in Toronto, the provincial capital.

Northwest Ontario, however, is significantly different. Here, dozens and dozens of lakes dot the remote and wooded countryside. Popular with hunters and fishermen, many of these lake areas are accessible only by floatplane or boat. This area has led to the rise of many lake camps such as the ones Gary frequented, which cater to sports men and women.

In this area, moose and bear roam the dense woods. Walleye, northern pike, and bass populate the waters. And loons—the provincial bird of Ontario—swim on the water while guests marvel at their calls.

This area was settled by Native Americans long before the Europeans came in the seventeenth century. By that time, the natives had divided themselves into the Iroquoian tribes of the South and the Algonquian tribes of the North and Northwest, including the Cree and the Ojibway people who lived in the northwest area that so attracted Gary.[3]

These first people probably lived by fishing and hunting the same animals hunted today. The name "Ontario," is from an Iroquoian word meaning "beautiful lake" or "beautiful water."[4]

Even today, visitors to this area can see the influence of the natives as well as the later influence of the fur traders and the Hudson Bay Company. Just across the bay and a few miles inland from where Gary and Matilda camped for so many years is an old trading post of the Hudson Bay Company. About five or six miles from the camp, Ojibway Indians still live on a reserve.

It was moose hunting that first attracted Gary to Canada. In the early days—before it was outlawed by Canada—Gary would locate a moose by plane, land the plane, and then hunt the moose down on foot.

By one account, Gary, along with fellow hunters John Vande Noord and Art Rus, once was driving along a Canadian highway when a moose crossed it. The men stopped the vehicle and shot the moose right in the middle of the road.

Another time, Gary and Art Rus spotted a moose lying along the shore, 300 yards away. They shot twelve times and put nine holes through that moose, according to Gary.

In Search of a Better Way
The Lives and Legacies of Gary and Matilda Vermeer
207

"When you have a moose shot down, you have a lot of work ahead of you. They weigh about 1,400 pounds," said Gary. "At first, we gutted and quartered them and put them in the airplane. That was hard work. Later, we took it all off the bone right away, and put it in thirty-pound packages and you could carry it right in [to the plane].

"Moose meat is as good as any. It's better than deer, we thought, more like beef."

Settling Into Camp

It's unclear exactly when Gary and Matilda started staying at the wilderness camp they frequented all those years. It likely was at least a few years after Gary started moose hunting. Perhaps it was on one of those hunting trips that Gary first ended up staying at Dave's Wilderness Camp, owned by Pella resident John Vande Noord. Or it may have been just Gary's connection with John, a hunting buddy, that drew him to the camp.

Matilda (on right) and Edith Van Gorp show off their catch of the day in June 1968.

In any case, it was after John Vande Noord bought the camp in the fall of 1963, that Gary was first at the camp. A sheep shearer and carpenter from Pella, John frequently hunted ducks and geese with Gary in the Pella area and later moose in Canada.

John was the third owner of the camp, known at that time as "Dave's Wilderness Camp." By the time he bought the camp, originally built in

1947, it was quite run down. John and his wife, Viola, started tearing down cabins that summer of 1964 and building new ones, hauling materials forty miles by boat.

Located on the 15,000-acre Lake Wabaskang in northwest Ontario, the wilderness camp is accessible only by floatplane or by boat. In 1978, the Vande Noords sold it to John Morgan, a hunter and fisherman from Illinois. John Morgan sold it in 1991 to Jerry and Sally Lundy, who owned and operated it through the 2004 season, the Vermeers' last year at that particular camp. The camp is now owned by Dave Peffley of South Bend, Indiana.

A three-hour drive north of International Falls, Minnesota, the camp is in a heavily wooded area of the province. It offered guests a simple—but not primitive—vacation experience in Canada's wilderness. Under the Lundys' management, generators provided the camp with electricity around-the-clock so the cabins had hot showers and flush toilets. Kitchens were equipped with propane cooking stoves. Temperatures were generally moderate in the summers, daytimes averaging in the mid-seventies and dipping into the mid-fifties in the evenings to provide pleasant sleeping weather.

Because the camp wasn't accessible by car, most visitors parked their vehicles at Perrault Falls—about fifteen miles south of the camp. Jerry Lundy met his guests there with his large motor boat and boated the remaining twenty minutes back to camp.

Perrault Falls offered camp guests a post office and two country grocery stores—the Vermeers often shopped at Dutchie's to get their supplies. The Vermeers also occasionally came into town to eat at the town's sole restaurant, the Sunset Restaurant.

Gary contributed to other vacationers' experience by giving free plane rides one night a week to any of the camp's other guests who hadn't ever done that before—a delight to the camp owner, who knew that it was great public relations for his camp.

At first, though, Gary and Matilda's trips to Canada probably were occasional, and initially, Gary wasn't even all that interested in fishing. In his earliest years there, he is said to have not even bothered putting his line in the water, but instead just watched the geese and ducks. But by the 1970s, Gary was regularly ferrying his guests to the Canadian wilderness. To each person he took, he offered a unique experience and a lifelong memory.

Gary always rose early, ready for an early breakfast before heading out to a remote lake.

One summer day in Canada, Ken and Lois Schepel, a Pella pastor and his wife, rose before dawn and headed in the floatplane to a distant lake to fish, as was the Vermeers' custom. At noon, they ate fresh walleye fried on shore. That day they saw a moose, and they traveled by boat to a connecting lake where they ran the rapids and gaped at a roaring waterfall they had earlier seen by plane. The day ended with Gary and Matilda making supper for the couple.

It was a day jam-packed with incredible experiences. "After a fifteen-hour day of being in the outdoors, Gary, in a most understated and unassuming way said 'I think we had a pretty good day.'"[5]

Ken Weller, former president of Central College in Pella, and his wife Shirely shared a trip to Canada with Gary and Matilda in 1976.

Our biggest memory relates to Gary's unmatched piloting skill at searching out a solitary moose standing in the lily pads of a remote lake far below and his thoughtfulness in giving passengers who would ask "Where? Where?" a much-improved view. His roaring, banking dives to treetop level were thrilling and much appreciated by most riders but a wee bit troublesome for others who found it difficult to survive swallowing their stomachs the third or fourth time he shouted "There's one!" and slammed the stick forward.

I finally ended up vomiting in my favorite felt fishing hat and sheepishly suggesting I probably could see them just as well from the higher altitude.[6]

Dale Van Donselaar remembers a July 1981 trip he won as a Vermeer employee. Another employee sat down accidentally on the side of the inflatable boat near shore, ending up with his feet in the air in about eighteen inches of water. "Gary started laughing until tears were rolling down his eyes."[7]

"We had the privilege of going to Canada fishing with Gary and Matilda during the summer of 1996," said Howard and Lola Vander Hart, friends of Mary Vermeer Andringa "Neither of us had ever been on a lake in Canada so this 'wilderness experience' was new to us. We were overwhelmed by the servant attitude of the Vermeers. Gary got the bait, prepared the boat, taught us how to fish, and cleaned and prepared the fish. We did get to do our own eating."[8]

Allan Beyer, a fellow Faith Church member, won't forget his July 1997 trip when Gary hooked his own rod and reel that had fallen overboard the year before.[9]

Four of Gary's guests had a particularly unforgettable experience. Rev. Henry Vermeer, then pastor of First Reformed Church of Pella and not a blood relative, wrote about it in an eightieth birthday tribute to Gary:

I shall never forget how thrilled I was to be invited to join you on one of your never-to-be-forgotten fishing trips to Vermeer Lake. It was the latter part of May 1969. Our party consisted of four fishermen: Dr. Stewart Kanis, a Mr. (Arnold) Van Zee, you, the pilot, and I, Rev. Vermeer.

As was Gary's custom, the men flew from Pella to Baudette, Minnesota. There, they transferred to a floatplane and taxied up the Rainy River. At that point, the floatplane started to list significantly.

The pilot wisely decided to investigate and headed for a landing dock. . . . As we approached the dock, Dr. Kanis very unwisely jumped into the river, thinking he would guide the plane into the dock. Quickly, Gary coiled a rope and threw it out toward the beleaguered doctor. Too short! Once again, Gary coiled the rope, and again too short. Then it happened—the whole plane tipped, and fuselage and all was beneath the surface of the water, with the exception of the pontoons and the three men who had managed to maneuver in such a way as to remain safely on the pontoons. The current on the river was moving rapidly, and soon started us on a float trip down the river. Then came the rescue operations as a couple of old salts who had been observing our plight took out after us in a motor boat and gathered us into their boat. Dr. Kanis had his own rescue team come to save him about the time when almost completely out of breath; he was ready to resign himself to death by drowning. What an experience! If ever I saw God's kind providential hand operated so clearly and unmistakable, it was on that morning in May. As I had watched him floating further and further from us, I prayed fervently and desperately that he might be kept afloat. And it happened! Praise the Lord!

. . . After the story hit the street [back in Pella], some wiseacre quipped, 'Just think, a Christian Reformed elder took a Reformed preacher and tried to make a Baptist out of him.'

Well, the Reformed preacher lived to tell the story. The following Sunday, I used this memorable episode as the basis of my morning sermon, and entitled it, "Saved by the Heavenly Pilot."[10]

That was a trip Gary wouldn't forget either. Nor would Matilda, back home in Pella.

"Gary called to tell me that they had tipped over," recalled Matilda. "I had to go to the dentist with that all on my mind."

"Later Rev. Vermeer went with us again, and he caught a nine-pound walleye," Gary recalled. "That was really unusual. Walleyes are really good eating."

Grandchildren Fish Every Summer

From the time they were five or six years old, each of Gary and Matilda's grandchildren went to Canada almost every year.

Twice, in 1986 and again in 1995, the entire family enjoyed fishing in Canada at the same time. Other years, Gary and Matilda enjoyed camping with just a few family members at a time. At first, the girl cousins flew up together for a special time with their grandparents, and the boy cousins flew up another time. Later, as school and job conflicts arose, the grandchildren went as their schedules permitted. Rarely, though, did they miss a year.

"There were summers in college when it would be tough to fit Canada in, but you'd know that Grandpa would be disappointed if you didn't go," said Mindi Vanden Bosch. "That was your special week with Grandma and Grandpa. . . . He didn't always talk—but when you were in the boat, there wasn't anything else to do but to talk."

The oldest grandchild, Christy Vermeer, figures she probably spent part of twenty summers in Canada. "For me, Canada was my grandpa and grandma time, but especially grandpa time," Christy said. "I don't love to fish—I never have—but I love being with my grandparents."

She isn't the only one. "I never really loved fishing, but I caught thousands of walleyes," said Jason Andringa.

Gary and his grandchildren Jason and Mindi show off their catch.

Canada was the place the grandchildren could connect with their grandfather because he was in his element. He was different somehow, than he was, say, in the factory.

"I once worked at Vermeer, and I'd see him in the hall and I'd say 'Hello!? This is Christy, remember me?'

"Canada was the place he was most relaxed and where I first realized he has a sense of humor," she added.

"I remember a time in Canada when my brother told a funny story right before we ate, and my grandpa prayed—but he started laughing again, and he couldn't finish the prayer," recalled Mindi.

As usual, these trips with grandchildren followed a routine. Christy always hoped for good flying weather, because she hated making the four-hour trip by car north from the Canadian border. On the other hand, her brother, David, dreaded the "very, very bumpy" ride on the floatplane from the border to the camp. "The vibrations made me nauseous."

Meanwhile, Cousin Jason was more interested in flying than fishing. "When I was seven, I was really into planes. Grandpa would put cushions on the right seat, and he'd let me fly. He'd point to a lake, and I'd fly to that. Then he'd point to another lake, and I'd fly there."

Catching sight of land was a welcome relief to some of Gary's passengers who were susceptible to motion sickness.

Like the trip, the days in camp generally followed a routine. Gary rose early—far earlier than the grandchildren wanted—and made breakfast. David and his cousin, Allison, often pumped water out of the floats on the plane in the morning.

The Vermeers seldom fished Lake Wabaskang where their camp was. Instead they preferred to fly to a distant lake—where few others, if any, ever fished. Sharp Lake, about sixty miles away, was a favorite. Lake Matilda—so named by Bob and Dale—was another.

So when the plane was ready, they took off—Gary at the controls and a grandchild seated next to him. Once airborne, it was that grandchild's job to pull up the rudder by tugging hard on a ring in the floor and put it on a hook. It was a difficult job.

Matilda sat behind Gary. Another grandchild sat beside her. A third grandchild might sit behind them in the cargo area on top the life jackets, bumped up against the fishing poles.

Once they landed, Gary cut the engines and opened his door. Matilda scooted out onto the float, grabbed a rope and then jumped onto the dock to secure the plane. "I remember having to do it once when it was windy," recalled Christy. "It's really hard to do."

"My grandpa would always joke what a good plane catcher she was," recalled Mindi.

Gary grabbed a boat that he kept stashed in the bush, put it in the lake, put on the motor, and the grandparents and their grandchildren headed out. Gary manned the boat while Matilda baited the hooks with minnows and took the fish off the hooks, using rags to help her hold on to the slippery northern. One time, however, they got to the remote lake and couldn't find the rags. It was one of the few times Jason remembers Grandma being upset with Grandpa.

"Gary, did you forget the rags?"

"Well, I must have if they're not in the boat."

"Now, Gary, surely you aren't so stupid to have left those on the dock."

Gary didn't reply.

Before lunch at Sharp Lake, Gary cleaned the fish on a table he had built between two trees, then fried the fish on a camp stove right at shore. "He did it the same way every time, which is like his personality," said Jason.

By two or three in the afternoon, they were back at their camp. Their day of fishing was over. "I didn't know for years that you could fish in the afternoon," Christy said.

By that time Gary was ready for a nap. Matilda cleaned fish or found other chores to keep busy, while the grandchildren played. Sometimes they tried to catch minnows off the dock. Other times they played Frisbee golf. They started at an equipment shed, threw the disc to the flagpole, then to a light post, then to a particular rock, then a wood pile. They had ten to fifteen "holes" before the last one, where they had to land the disc on a glider-swing.

If they had fish for dinner, Gary usually fried it. If not, Matilda cooked. On occasion, they went out to dinner. They motored in their small metal fishing boat to eat in Perrault Falls—a 45-minute trip—at the Sunset Restaurant.

After dinner, they played cards for a while. Rook was a favorite. "Grandpa and Grandma usually won. Whatever card Grandpa needed, Grandma had it. It was uncanny," Christy said. Early—perhaps by 8:00—Gary was ready for bed. The grandchildren usually stayed up later, talking, reading, and playing cards.

Finding a Better Way in Canada

The cabin the Vermeers rented was comfortable but simple—three bedrooms, a combined kitchen and living room area, and a bathroom. Every year, Gary rented the same cabin, Cabin No. 4—until 1994.

"In 1994 someone else was in the cabin, and Grandpa didn't like that, so Grandpa built his own cabin," recalled David, who sees that as a typical reaction of his grandfather. "If he doesn't like something or the way something is done, he'll build his own."

In Search of a Better Way
The Lives and Legacies of Gary and Matilda Vermeer
217

In August of that year, Gary told Jerry Lundy he wanted exclusive use of cabin No. 4 for the following year, even during those weeks when he wouldn't be at the camp. Jerry couldn't do that, he said. So Gary countered by saying that they needed to build another cabin. At first, Jerry balked, but eventually relented.

That was a summer before Jason was to start pre-law courses at Calvin College. "After I built a cabin with Grandpa in Canada, and I enjoyed working with him so much, I decided to try engineering at Calvin."

It was a project that Jerry, and just about everyone else at the camp that August, had a hand in, Jerry recalled. It had to be built in a hurry. Jerry knew it had to be finished that fall so that it was ready for Gary at the start of the following season.

Jason and his grandfather took a boat out to fetch sand for the cement for the cabin's pilings. "My grandpa figured out how many buckets of sand we could take in the boat [without swamping it]. He just did that in his head."

That was far from the only time Gary used his ingenuity in Canada.

Early one morning, Gary was at Jason's bedside urgently trying to wake him up: "Jason, get up! Jerry's dock is floating away!"

Hastily, Jason got dressed and joined his grandfather outside. The wind had come up so strong during the night that the wind was catching the tail of their floatplane tied up at the dock. The wind was pushing the plane and the dock with it. Jason waded out with a rope to secure the floatplane better. But it was only a temporary solution.

"Grandpa figured out how to get an old engine housing to the front of the dock to use as an anchor," said Jason. Some were skeptical that Gary would ever be able to haul the engine block out there to make it work, but Gary figured out the solution quickly in his head. It worked.

"We were always fiddling with things," Jason added. If the generator quit, or a door handle on the plane broke, somehow Gary figured out a way to jury-rig something to make it work.

There is one of Gary's inventions that Jerry Lundy has never forgotten.

It happened the year that Jerry put in floating docks at the campsite. "Gary always said the biggest improvement was when I put in the floating docks," he recalled. "Gary always said that's the one he appreciated the most."

While these docks worked great during the summer, Jerry and Gary both knew they would have to be removed over the winter before the frozen lake broke them apart. Getting them out wasn't going to be easy.

"Gary came up to me and said, 'How are you going to get those out?'" Jerry, who figures he invested $12,000 to $15,000 to build those docks, certainly wasn't going to let the ice break them up. "I don't know—blood, sweat, and tears—but I'll get them out."

Grandson Jonathan remembers what happened next. "So Grandpa out of the goodness of his heart created a contraption, a trailer kind of thing with pulleys on it, to make a much easier and safer way to get the docks out."

Gary went home to Pella, built the trailer, and shipped it to Canada. Jerry and Sally Lundy were very grateful. "It wasn't good enough for Gary just to make the trailer," Jerry said, "Gary and Matilda drove all the way from Pella, Iowa, to the camp just to help us take the docks out of the water. After Gary was satisfied that his trailer would do the job, he packed up and went home.[11]

Gary, frying fish for a shore lunch at Sharp Lake.

"Unbelievable. That is Gary and Matilda right to a T."

In 2005, Gary went to Canada for his last time. That year, the family stayed at a different camp. Tall Pines Camp was also on Lake Wabaskang, just north of Perrault Falls, but unlike the other camp, was accessible by road. By this time, Gary was eighty-six years old, and walking had become difficult for him.

Granddaughter Allison Van Wyngarden and her husband Kyle went to Canada that year. "It was a bittersweet trip. He couldn't do the things he wanted to do.

"It was the right time to be done with Canada."

Gary and Matilda on the Hawaiian beach, 1958

8 An Adventurous Spirit

I appreciate the part of him that likes to explore. . . . I appreciate his sense of adventure, of doing it differently."

~ Christy Vermeer, oldest grandchild

It probably wouldn't be going too far out on a limb to say that of all the Iowa farmers raised during the Depression, Gary and Matilda are among the most traveled.

Why did they travel so much? What motivated them?

The couple traveled to all fifty states, around the world several times, to all seven continents at least twice, to nearly a dozen African countries, and even to the North Pole.

Part of it was clearly opportunity. Their finances allowed them to afford the trips. With dealers all over the country and the world, Gary had people he could visit. Their strong Dutch heritage was reason enough to visit the Netherlands and also other areas where the Dutch had immigrated. Missionaries they knew gave them a reason to visit remote areas.

But somehow opportunity isn't a satisfactory answer. Many people have the opportunity to travel, but find other things that call for their time.

The Vermeers were no different in that respect, but Gary wouldn't always heed that call.

Even his grandchildren knew how the typical conversation might go. At a celebration of Gary and Matilda's fiftieth wedding anniversary, grandchildren Allison and David parodied such a conversation:

Gary: "Let's go see the polar bears."

Matilda: "But Gary, I have twelve things to do tomorrow."

"You know Grandpa," the grandchildren concluded. "He says, 'That's no problem!' and off they go."[1]

Grandson Jonathan Vermeer offered this explanation: "I think he loved new experiences, cultures, and nature. He loved to see animals and scenery. Specific things interested him, and they often involved the outdoors or some engineering marvel."

Many who travel extensively have thrill-seeker traits. That really isn't the case with Gary or Matilda. Yes, Gary often piloted himself and his family on his domestic travels. Yes, the couple toured places most of us never seriously consider. And yes, the couple has ridden an elephant in India and a camel by the Egyptian pyramids.

But danger and daring were not the driving force. "The key is the adventure," said Lois Vermeer. "He would rather do something on the edge of what humanity is doing, like visit Antarctica and the North Pole."

"Frontiersman" is perhaps the best descriptor.

Trips Inspired by Missionaries

Many of Gary and Matilda's trips resulted from involvement in their church. They are members of the Christian Reformed church, a Protestant denomination that adheres to Calvinist theology and finds its roots in the Dutch Reformed tradition in the Netherlands. In particular, the missionaries of this church influenced Gary and Matilda's travels.

"Gary and Matilda often made a bedroom available to missionaries when they came. Gary was fascinated by the world. He said, 'I'm going to visit you when you are back in your country.' This gave him a local connection," said Mary Andringa.

In 1958, while many Americans were more concerned about the Cold War or the race into space or even getting their first color television set, Gary and Matilda made their first trip to Nigeria. They left their three children behind in Pella.

They visited Dr. Larry Den Besten at the Takum Christian Hospital. A native of Pella, Larry had been in the same grade in school as Gary's younger brother, Harry. Larry spent nine years as a medical missionary in Nigeria. Besides serving as medical director at the Takum Christian Hospital, he also was medical director and chief of surgery at the Mkar Hospital.

Nigeria, on the west coast of Africa, is about a third larger than Texas and is the most populous country in Africa. While English is the official language, more

Matilda and Mary at an orphanage in Nigeria

than 500 local languages are spoken. When Gary and Matilda first visited the country, it was still under British rule. In 1960, it gained its independence, but by 1966, the first of a series of military dictators took over.

On their trip in 1958, Gary and Matilda flew into Jos, Nigeria, a city near the center of the country located on a plateau that made its temperatures more moderate and its vegetation more abundant. From there, Gary and Matilda traveled by car to Mkar, a 260-mile trip mostly over dirt roads. They visited a missionary hospital there.

From Mkar, they continued traveling by car to Takum. Again, it was a long drive on a road heavy with dust. On the way, they crossed the Katsina-Ala River by ferry. "By the time we got there, everything was just covered with red dust!" said Matilda.

The difficult trip prompted the Vermeers to come up with a better transportation plan for the mission. Working through an unusually large amount of red tape, the Vermeers donated a plane to Christian Reformed World Missions for this purpose.

Nigeria became a place that grew in importance to the family. In 1964, after graduating from Calvin College, Stan, Gary and Matilda's oldest son, spent a year teaching in Nigeria. After a year of study in Israel, followed by studies at Calvin Theological Seminary where he obtained his degree, Stan and his wife, Margaret, returned to Nigeria, where they taught at the Bristow Secondary School, a school established in 1960 by Christian Reformed World Missions and named for missionary William Muckle Bristow. The couple stayed in Nigeria until April 1974.

So, it wasn't surprising that during the Christmas season in 1964, Gary and Matilda—this time joined by their other children, Bob and Mary—made their second trip to Nigeria to visit Stan. Gary and Matilda made additional trips to the country in 1967 and 1973.[2]

Round and Round the World

Gary at Angkor Wat in 1963

The couple went around the world at least three times, the first time in 1963.

One of the sites most etched in Gary's memory from their first world tour is Angkor Wat in northwestern Cambodia. It is one of more than 100 temples of Angkor, the seat of the ancient and vast Khmer Empire. Khmer kings ruled over an area that today would stretch from Vietnam to China to the Bay of Bengal.[3]

Angkor Wat was built over a period of thirty years in the early twelfth century by King Suryavarman II, and honors the Hindu god, Vishnu. The enormous temple includes five towers, believed to represent the five peaks of Mount Meru—the mythical home of the gods.

It was an engineering masterpiece and one of Gary's favorite sites. "It had a temple a mile square! Trees had grown up all through it," Gary recalled more than forty years after his 1963 visit. "It was really an interesting place to see—what they had done so long ago."

"We saw so many temples, we got sick and tired of it," recalled Matilda. "After a while, we didn't go inside some of them."

It was probably on that trip in 1963 that the Vermeers visited Rev. Cornie De Bruin, who served as a missionary in India for many years. Like Larry Den Besten, he was a Pella native.

Also on that 1963 trip, the Vermeers visited South Korea where they saw Dr. Peter and Eleanor Boelens. Peter, a Calvin College alumni, worked as a medical evangelist in Korea setting up clinics and helping establish fifteen churches. He later founded Cary Christian Center, a medical ministry in Cary, Mississippi, and then became executive director of the Luke Society, an interdenominational organization of Christian health and business professionals dedicated to medical missions.

What the Vermeers remember most clearly about that trip was the Seoul fish market. The fish were in buckets for people to buy. And merchants sold live chickens; the buyers had to butcher them. The Boelens, however, best remember the ride from the airport where they picked up the Vermeers. "Gary must have taken twenty pictures out the car window of men riding bicycles with a live pig tied on the back," said Eleanor Boelens. "He thought that was the funniest thing. Of course, private cars were nonexistent in those days, so there were a lot of bicycles."

It was also on that trip that Matilda became very homesick. Her youngest child, Mary, was only fourteen years old then, and Matilda wasn't quite comfortable leaving her for so long. In fact, Matilda became so homesick that the Vermeers ended their trip early. They had scheduled a three-month round-the-world package with a tour group. But the Vermeers left the tour ten days early.

At least on one of the trans-world trips, the Vermeers flew from Johannesburg, South Africa, to Perth, Australia—"the most beautiful city in the world," according to Gary. Once in Australia, Gary called on the Vermeer dealer. "I told our dealer I wanted to go to the outback. He said no one wants to go to the outback. But he had an uncle who had six sheep shearing crews and he took us to the outback." They took along extra gas, because there weren't any gas stations. And they saw plenty of sheep as well as kangaroos.

Some of these trips Gary and Matilda took alone; others they were joined by family or friends such as Bob and Harriet Zylstra, and Hillie and Art Rus. Many were an organized tour of some kind.

On a trip through parts of Africa with the Zylstras, they encountered a man named Amani who was saving money for a bride price. He liked American money, he told them. Of course, the group gave him some.

"In Ethiopia, they got really testy about our visa being one day off. We were the only white people in the airport. It really gave you a feeling of being a minority," said Harriet Zylstra. "Gary contacted Sudan United Missions, and they sent someone who got us through."

Gary and Matilda in Egypt in 1963

On that same trip in Africa, it seemed as if everywhere they went, they were served the same cream soup. It always had a different name, but it had the same base, maybe a few carrots or beets thrown in occasionally. "There must be a big barrel of it just following us around the continent," the couples joked.

The family's memories of these international trips have faded over the years, and what remains are mostly small snapshots of some of the details: visiting the Taj Mahal; riding camels by the Egyptian pyramids; traveling to an East African game park in 1967; visiting the Holy Land; and eating dinner with author James Michener en route to Antarctica in 1980.

Hiking Grand Canyon at Seventy

When Gary and Matilda hiked with their family down the Grand Canyon and back, Gary was seventy and Matilda was sixty-nine. The youngest grandchild, David, had just turned seven.

Family members wondered whether the family patriarch and matriarch would have the stamina to hike down the canyon one entire day and hike back up the next. As it turned out, Gary and Matilda—who walked frequently their entire lives—managed well. That trip was at least their fifth down the canyon. They arrived early this time so they could walk halfway down and back up again to be sure they could still do it.

"Our parents were struggling, but Grandma and Grandpa were fine, and the grandkids, of course, were fine," said Christy.

Gary and Matilda had trained for the trip on a hill three or four miles north of Pella. "They would walk up and down that hill ten times just to get in shape," said Stan.

"The first time we practiced we got so stiff," said Matilda. "It was painful going down a few steps to the restaurant to eat with John and Effie [Gary's brother and his wife] after that first walk. But after that we never had that."

To tackle the Grand Canyon, the Vermeers had a plan. Gary would take the lead and set the pace. Everyone else was to follow. Dale Andringa would bring up the rear. Even the grandkids weren't to run ahead. Gary counted the steps and stopped every 100 to 200 steps, depending on how steep it was, Stan said. "He counted the paces. He would stop and say 'Now, does anyone need to rest?'"

"That kept everyone under control. Then people would stand

Gary and Matilda joined their family to hike down and back up the Grand Canyon in 1989.

around and chat and yuck it up. That is typical of how he approached life. He approached the Grand Canyon in a very structured way," recalled Dale Andringa.

The family followed the Bright Angel trail on the way down, a nine-and-one-half mile trek that descends 4,400 feet. It is listed as a "strenuous" trail by the American Park Network. Along the way, they frequently had to yield the right of way to the mules that less physically adventurous explorers rode down the canyon. The hikers also had to be on the lookout for the droppings the mules left behind.

"We did Bright Angel on the way down and I thought, 'How could the other one possibly be steeper?' I would see a wall with tiny people all over it, and I thought, 'My gosh, I have to climb that and it is straight up!'" said Dale. "It was amazing."

At the bottom of the canyon, they stayed at Phantom Ranch. The grandchildren played horseshoes and other games. "We could hardly walk, and the kids went and played," said Dale.

In the morning, after a hot breakfast, they were handed a sack lunch and started their way up the canyon, this time on the Kaibab Trail—a six-and-one-half hour trek that the American Park Network describes as "very strenuous." Though the views are fabulous, "the South Kaibab Trail is steep, dropping close to 5,000 feet in 6.3 miles."[4]

For the Vermeer family, that meant climbing 5,000 feet in 6.3 miles.

Fiftieth Anniversary Safari

In 1989, while the family was celebrating a family birthday at Pella's Strawtown Inn, the topic of Gary and Matilda's fiftieth wedding anniversary coming up in

1991 came into the conversation. Stan suggested celebrating by taking a safari to Africa. Not all family members were initially enthusiastic, but in the end, all of them went.

The group flew into Kenya, then traveled into Tanzania where they began their safari at the Ngorongoro Crater, which has been called "Africa's Eden" and even the "Eighth Natural Wonder of the World." The crater, called a caldera, is a collapsed volcano twelve miles in diameter that teems with wildlife.[5]

David, Allison, and Mindi with the Masai tribe at Ngorongoro. The Vermeers' guide, Chris Michaelides, is standing behind David.

The family spent a full day touring the crater floor in four-wheel-drive Land Rovers. At the bottom, they met several members of the Masai tribe, an indigenous tribe allowed to live within the protected area. "They were ready to have their pictures taken with us, for a fee!" Christy wrote in the scrapbook she made of that trip. "They had learned to profit from tourism."

After leaving the crater, the Vermeers traveled to the Lobo Wildlife Lodge, built among large boulders in the Serengeti National Park. Christy remembered it as "one of the most memorable of our places to stay. The views were fantastic from the bedrooms, and there was the sound of the baboons running across the roofs.

Some observed a baboon taking the purse of a guest (not one of us) and open it and then start to scatter it as he was running away." The Serengeti National Park is world-famous because of the 1½ million wildebeests that roam and migrate within the park.

The family also toured Lake Manyara National Park where they watched giraffes sparring by knocking their heads together.

Gary and Matilda enjoyed providing new sights for their family.

This trip was all about the wildlife. And Gary, who takes great pleasure in seeing all wildlife, must have been delighted to share his appreciation with his family. The trip started when the family spotted the greater bustard, and continued with silver-backed jackals, crested cranes, a pride of lions, flamingoes, hippos, a black rhino with its baby, zebras, Thompson's gazelles, wildebeests, impalas, wart hogs, monkeys, baboons, elephants, crocodiles, spotted hyenas, giraffes, a rock hyrax, an agama lizard, cheetahs, storks, red hornbills, wild dogs, and still more.

On July 12, the family was back in Nairobi, Kenya, having dinner at the Carnivore restaurant, eating zebra and hartebeest (a kind of antelope).

Of course, flying halfway across the world does have its hassles. The airline lost Gary and Matilda's luggage on that trip. So Matilda bought a few necessities and a safari camouflage suit, packing all their things into a carry-on bag. "They got along with so little for the trip, as we all lugged large suitcases everywhere," Lois recalled. Before Matilda left Africa, she gave away her camouflage suit.

"Incidentally, their luggage was found on the way back," Lois added. "[The suitcases] were broken into and almost everything was gone. But Gary and Matilda took it all in stride."

For the Vermeers, the safari was an opportunity that even they, as well-traveled as they are, won't ever forget. Just what Gary intended. "I think Grandpa has a sense of satisfaction, a happiness that his family was with him," said Christy. "He'd done it before, but he really enjoyed sharing it with his family. I think he enjoyed watching us enjoy it."

Christy described the trip as "exhilarating—seeing amazing things with some of my favorite people."

Boating in Antarctica

In 1996, Gary made his second and last trip to Antarctica. He took Matilda; his brother John and his wife, Effie; his son Stan and his wife, Alma, and their children, Christy, Jonathan, and David; his grandson Jason; and Marvin and Betty Bruxvoort. Marvin had farmed with or for Gary since 1957.

The previous spring, Jonathan, in his last semester at Wheaton College, had been startled one morning when his grandfather called him out of the blue. Not one to talk much on the phone, Gary got straight to the point. "I want to let you know that Grandma and I want to take a trip to Antarctica and take anyone who wants to go."

Christy, in Colorado, was similarly surprised by a call from her grandfather that April. "I never had him call me before, and I'm thinking, 'Who is this?'" She was even more surprised by the invitation to Antarctica. "It's never been on my list of places to visit, and I don't like the cold, but I said, 'Okay.'"

And her conversation with her grandfather was over.

Like the rest of the Vermeer grandchildren, Jonathan can be considered a world traveler. He said the Antarctica trip was "probably the best trip of my life."

The Vermeers and Bruxvoorts left Des Moines on December 16 for Miami, where they were joined by Jason, on his college Christmas break. From there, the group flew on to Buenos Aires.

After a day in Argentina's capital city, they flew to Ushuaia where they spent another day. Ushuaia, the capital of the Argentine province of Tierra del Fuego, is the southernmost city in the world. Surrounded by mountains, the small city is home to about 50,000 people. While there, some of the family hiked to a glacier behind the hotel. Others spent the morning about seven miles outside the city at the Tierra Del Fuego National Park, where David, a horticultural enthusiast, was especially pleased to find several types of miniature orchids.[6]

It was in Ushuaia that the Vermeers and Bruxvoorts boarded the Russian ship, the Alla Tarasova, named after a Russian actress especially popular in the 1920s and 1930s. Having a reinforced hull, the ship was often put into service for trips to the Arctic and Antarctica. It was nothing fancy. As Jonathan said, "It was appropriate for my grandfather. It was functional and practical." Jonathan, who had been in Russia on a missions trip the previous summer, welcomed the chance to try out the few Russian words he had learned with the Russian staff members.

The boat carried about eighty passengers, who had unusually free reign of the ship. They could go almost anywhere, even up to the bridge.

From Ushuaia, the Alla Tarasova—accompanied by albatrosses and petrels—traveled for two days along the Drake Passage, the body of water between the tip of South America and the South Shetland Islands of Antarctica. Along the way, the ship crossed the Antarctic Convergence, a name that refers to a varying line that circles Antarctica where the cold waters from the south merge with the warmer waters from the Atlantic. These waters are among the most turbulent in the world.

The high number of nutrients in these waters creates a large concentration of marine life, which also tends to create more animal life.[7]

Aboard ship, Gary and Matilda and their guests often took in the naturalists' presentations about wildlife or topography. Other times, they played cards and watched the unusual scenery.

At mealtimes, all the ship's passengers ate at the same time. While their grandparents tended to eat with family members or with the Bruxvoorts, Jonathan and Jason particularly liked to eat with guests at other tables. "The types of people who go on these trips tend to be really interesting," said Jonathan. He liked to hear stories of their trips.

By the evening of December 21, the ship arrived at the South Shetland Islands. At 10 p.m., the group made its first landing at the Arctowski Station, a Polish research station located at Admiralty Bay on King George Island.[8] Zodiacs, motorized inflatable boats capable of holding twelve people, carried the passengers to the island.

In December, that part of the earth is tilted toward the sun, which means the area is covered with sun nearly round the clock. So at 10 p.m., the group had no problem seeing the elephant seals and adelie penguins in the area.

The wildlife they saw there and elsewhere throughout their trip was spectacular. On Rongo Island, they explored a gentoo penguin rookery, where they saw hundreds of penguins in their nests. Gentoo penguins, distinctive with their bright orange beak, stand about thirty to thirty-five inches tall. At nesting time, they use stones, grass, sticks, or anything else they can find to build their circular nests. When nest-building, gentoos have been known to fight over stones or even steal stones from other nests.[9]

Besides the gentoo penguins, they saw chinstrap penguins and adelie penguins, which at twenty-eight inches tall, are the smallest penguins in Antarctica. They saw king cormorants, hourglass dolphins, and crabeater seals, which actually eat krill, not crab.

At the British research station, Port Lockroy, on the Antarctic Peninsula, the group watched for at least twenty minutes while a returning penguin mate danced and called to prove he was the correct mate and the one to take the next turn sitting on the nest.

"I thought she would never accept him," Christy wrote in her scrapbook. "But then, very quickly she moved off and he moved on. The switch must be done quickly, or else the waiting skuas [seabirds that look like large dark gulls with sharp claws] will steal the eggs."[10]

In Paradise Bay, the travelers spotted humpback whales. Passengers boarded zodiacs and were among five or six humpback whales. "One surfaced fifteen feet from the boat. You could smell the breath. It was exciting," said Jonathan.

In Search of a Better Way
The Lives and Legacies of Gary and Matilda Vermeer
237

Zodiaks took the family for a closer look at the humpback whales and other wildlife.

Matilda tells it a bit differently. "Jason and Jon went out with a boat. I was worried the whales would come up under the boat. There were whales everywhere!"

"We kept cruising, never quite sure where the whales would surface next. Fortunately for us they were feeding slowly, working along a sub-marine ledge, not bothered by us at all. The whales could easily have flipped us, but they didn't," said Christy. "We were blessed with three and one-half hours of whale watching."[11]

Besides the wildlife, the scenery was unlike any other in the world. "The water and the ice really are blue," Christy wrote. "The variety of ice formations is incredible."[12]

At Neke Harbour, the ship made its second continental landing. "We were truly fortunate. Some never even make it once," said Christy. Poor weather sometimes prevented ships from landing.

On Antarctica, the travelers spent some time on the land, enjoying the view, and hiked to a ridge to get a better view. They walked on soft snow, packed snow, and sometimes exposed rock and earth. Throughout the trip, the temperature was generally around freezing. One day, however, it got into the forties and the snow was soft. Jonathan, Jason and some other young passengers found it perfect for a snowball fight.

The Vermeers enjoy a calm day on the sea, which at times is the roughest in the world.

On Christmas Day, daylong storms set in, making another landing impossible. The Vermeer group stayed indoors all day, mostly attending lectures and playing Rook. Jason called home. The family gathered in a lounge to exchange small presents. Matilda received a sweatshirt that said, "Need a Hug, call 1-800-Grandma."

To celebrate that day, the ship provided hot mulled wine. "I never saw my grandparents drink—ever," Jonathan said, but that day they tried a sip. "They weren't judgmental and they didn't care if anyone else drank."

A week earlier when the Vermeer party had headed south along the Drake Passage, the waters were rough as they usually were, but this time, on their return trip north, the waters proved treacherous.

Passengers had to hold on to something secure to keep from slipping to the other side of the deck or the room as the ship rocked. If passengers wanted to move to the other side, they first held on to their own side, then waited for the ship to pitch so that they could run down the slope to the other side where they grabbed something to keep themselves upright before the boat pitched back again.

On the bridge—probably fifty feet above the water—Jason and Jonathan watched waves splash over the entire boat.

With the possible exception of Jason—who never seems to suffer motion sickness—the entire group took some seasickness pills. When Matilda stopped taking them for a couple days, she got very sick and was especially glad to get back to Ushuaia.

After a six-hour delay at Ushuaia, the group finally made it back to Buenos Aires where they toured the city. They saw historical sites, a flea market, the brightly painted houses of fishermen, an artist at work, the National Cemetery, Juan and Eva Peron's family tomb, and celebrated their trip with a farewell steak dinner.[13]

North Pole at Last

In August 2001, while the rest of their family was traveling in Greece, Gary and Matilda went to the North Pole. It was their first time there. Or, as Gary said in his own wry way: "2001 was our first and only time. You don't go there very often."

The couple flew to New York, where they caught a plane for Oslo, Norway. "It was a beautiful city," Gary recalled. The streets by their motel were just as clean as they could be. They spent a night in Oslo and also went to Spitzbergen, an island off Norway.

At eighty degrees north, Spitzbergen is inside the Arctic Circle and is the largest island of a group of islands called Svalbard. In June, the sun shines twenty-four hours a day. Mountains, covered with snow, loom above the ice-covered ground. This is home to the auk, a black and white bird, and the white and gray kittiwake, so named because of its distinct kittee-wa-aaake call.

To make the trip to the North Pole, the Vermeers traveled on a Russian ice breaker—a ship with a pointed end to help break up ice encountered on the way. Matilda described it as "old and rugged."

"It was a tough little boat," said Gary. "It would just plow through that ice. There is a lot of ice there in the middle of the summer. It was unbelievable how that thing would go through the ice. It was noisy." Gary smiled, remembering.

Nothing like a cruise ship, the boat was rugged and simple, built to handle about ninety passengers. "They served us good food, and took good care of us. We had a cabin, a pretty nice room, with bunk beds. We didn't have much room to take anything along," said Gary.

Along the way, they saw many northern birds as well as polar bears and walruses. The temperature, generally around thirty degrees, was cold but not uncomfortable. And most days were sunny. "We had coveralls on, and could handle it easy," said Gary.

On board, they mostly listened to lectures and watched the scenery. They liked to stand up in the pointed front of the boat and watch the ice split. "There were times we couldn't make it, and we would back up and try again," Gary said.

Despite the fact that the tour was organized by Iowa State University, and their tour guide was from Iowa State, Gary and Matilda were the only people from Iowa making the trip.

Other passengers included people from Pennsylvania, a police officer from New York— "he didn't even own a car!" said Matilda—and a ninety-two-year-old southern gentleman, perhaps from Georgia. "He was alone. He didn't have a wife anymore, if he ever had one," recalled Matilda. "I sat next to him once. He didn't have any socks on, just his shoes. Now I know why. If you are alone when you are old, you can hardly get socks on."

Ice alternated with open water, but more ice predominated. At ninety degrees latitude—the North Pole—the ship's captain parked the vessel so passengers

In 2001, Gary and Matilda made it to the North Pole.

could take a dip into the water if they wished. Some did, including the ninety-two-year-old man.

A dip in the frigid water didn't particularly interest Gary and Matilda. "A dozen went into the water. We weren't that close, and the walking was uneven, so we didn't go down there," said Matilda.

The North Pole has long carried a mystique that has lured adventurers in the same way that its most famous resident, Santa Claus, has captivated children around the globe. As early as the 1820s, adventurers have been seeking to reach the pole. Most accounts credit American Robert Edwin Peary as the first explorer to reach the pole in 1909.[14]

Almost a century after that famous expedition, Gary, nearly 83 years old, and Matilda, 81, had reached the top of the world.

On the Road, In the Air. . .

Trips to Antarctica, the North Pole, the Grand Canyon, Australia, and Africa were among the larger and more memorable trips that Gary and Matilda took. But over the years, they took hundreds more—big and small.

Gary and Matilda with their children and grandchildren at the Tanque Verde Ranch in Tucson.

Early trips include Lake Okoboji in Iowa, Christmas in Fort Lauderdale in 1956, and Washington, D.C., in 1957. Gary and Matilda visited Hawaii in 1957, before it was a state. A year later, the family traveled to California. In 1960, the family went to Alaska. That same year, Stan and Gary traveled to Cuba—just a little over a year after Fidel Castro led the revolution, successfully overthrowing Fulgencio Batista and about two-and one-half years before the Cuban Missile Crisis.

Trips to visit dealers were combined with family trips to nearby sites. The Vermeers took trips to conventions and meetings. They took trips to Tucson's Tanque Verde Ranch where, according to Gary, "when you walked in the timber, the coyotes would be howling right next to you."

They took trips to see Allison in horse shows and to see Mindi in basketball games. They traveled to California to see Jonathan and Jason for the five years they both lived there. They flew to Michigan to visit grandchildren and great grandchildren.

And, in addition to the summer trips to Canada fishing, the couple traveled at least three times to their Canadian camp in the winter.

One such trip was spurred by a conversation. It was in the 1960s when Gary telephoned Pella residents John and Viola Vande Noord, who owned the camp at that time.

"I wonder how much snow there is on the ground up at the camp?" Gary asked John.

John said he didn't know.

"Do you want to go up and see?"

So Gary, Matilda, John, and Viola flew to Baudette, Minnesota, in Gary's plane that same day. There, Gary rented a floatplane with skis to fly to the camp where he landed on the ice-covered lake. They hiked around the camp, built a fire in the fireplace of the one cabin that was always left unlocked, ate some sandwiches, and flew home again that same day.

"That's the way Gary was. He liked to do things on the spur of the moment," said Viola. "That day was the most fun I ever had up there."

Gary went back at least two other times to the camp over winter. In 1998, Gary and Matilda, along with Jerry and Sally Lundy, the camp owners at the time, rented snowmobiles to get into the camp. In 2000, the Lundys again rode snowmobiles into the camp while Gary and Matilda rented a ski plane that took them into the remote camp.

Driving a snowmobile was fun for Matilda. She remembers driving snowmobiles around Yellowstone in the winter—and driving through a half-dozen buffalo.

As recently as July 2007, the couple went to Yellowstone. Son Stan drove and they picked up Granddaughter Christy in Colorado Springs on the way. By this time, Gary was nearly 89 and had suffered some health problems that summer, but he refused to stop traveling. He saw Old Faithful once again. "We saw hundreds of buffalo. Some elk, not many, and a few bear, but hundreds of buffalo," said Gary.

"They were tame," added Matilda. "A big buffalo came right between our car and the one next to us. They weren't afraid."

Some of these trips carried a big price tag. The North Pole trip may have cost as much as $40,000 for the two of them. The African Safari probably cost at least $1,000 per person—not counting airfare. Seventeen were on that trip, including future in-law Tricia Vander Waal, invited by Gary when Grandson Dan considered skipping the trip to spend more time that summer with her.

Obviously, Gary and Matilda could afford these trips. But they were frugal people, and though they spent money on the travel, the couple generally remained true to their nature.

If they flew commercial, they flew coach. If they went out to dinner, McDonald's or Denny's were their restaurants of choice. If they stayed in a motel, they preferred one of the less expensive chain motels.

"On vacations, they didn't do anything extravagant," said Jonathan. "We usually stayed at Super 8s or even Motel 6s, but at the same time, my grandfather would be willing to spend money for unique experiences.

In Search of a Better Way
The Lives and Legacies of Gary and Matilda Vermeer
245

"Amenities were not an issue for him," Jonathan added. "He didn't need a spa or marble floors. It was all about the experience."

"I appreciate his love of nature and am glad he's exposed us to that in various ways, whether it's Canada or a Safari or Antarctica," said Christy.

Gary and Matilda have seen polar bears lounging at the North Pole and humpback whales surfacing near Antarctica. They have watched giraffes sparring in Tanzania, moose drinking the clean water in Canada, and sheep being sheared in Australia's outback.

As Gary might say, that's pretty good for a farmer from Iowa.

*Harry, Gary, and Ralph were on the board
when the Foundation was first created.*

9 Giving to the Community

The first year in business, the company made $44,000. We thought we should give some money away. Kenny Bean at Marion County State Bank said, 'If you want to give some away, I will loan it to you.' We borrowed $4,000 to give away.

~ Gary Vermeer[1]

Gary's community involvement as president of Vermeer Manufacturing Company began with a debt. Because of the company's cash flow at the time, the company didn't have any cash on hand to donate for charitable purposes. As a result, Gary compromised his strict no-debt principles to borrow money to give away.

"We had a good profit and no money—we had accounts receivable, inventory, but no cash," Gary recalled in 2007. "So we went to the bank and said we wanted to donate money because we had made quite a bit."

That proved to be the genesis of the Vermeer Foundation. Exactly when the idea first came up to begin a foundation isn't clear, but according to Gary, Glenn Andreas first broached the idea. Glenn, then president of Pella National Bank, was a good friend of Gary's business partner and cousin, Ralph Vermeer.

Almost ten years to the day after Ralph and Gary signed the articles of incorporation for Vermeer Manufacturing Company, the company established the Foundation. At a November 24, 1958, meeting, the Vermeer board of directors formally established the Vermeer Foundation with an initial contribution of $100.[2]

The Vermeer Charitable Foundation has helped people around the globe.

From the beginning, the Foundation said its purpose was to relieve poverty, advance education, promote health, and extend the influence of religion. Gary, Ralph, and Gary's brother, Harry, made up the board with Gary apparently as the head. From the start, the board adopted a policy to contribute annually the maximum tax-deductible amount for charitable giving allowed by the IRS.[3]

"It has been a pretty good thing. If you have a pot somewhere, it is easier to give away," said Gary.

Today, the company generally puts about five percent of its profit into the Vermeer Charitable Foundation, figuring the specific percentage after year-end bonuses are given to employees. In this way, the company is fair to its employees: the shareholders—not the employees—bear the brunt of the contributions. In addition, the company contributed to the Foundation the royalties it received from its round baler patent.

Deciding What to Fund

How has the family decided over the years what to fund? Although family members have struggled deciding which of the many worthwhile projects it should fund, Gary answers this question in a simpler way. "That isn't hard to do," said Gary. "You just give it away."

His children say his motives have been altruistic. "Making the community a better place for its people has been an important thing for Gary," said Mary Andringa.

Stan Vermeer describes his father's philosophy about the Foundation as similar to his philosophy concerning his business. "Dad looks and says, 'Okay, there are needs, and what can I do to make a difference in meeting that need?' When he saw needs, he tried to make it happen. He saw the challenge in what had not been done before. He saw a need for the hospital, for an indoor swimming pool, for a nursing home, and then he worked at meeting those needs."

As the Foundation brochure says: "Vermeer has found success in seeing a need and filling that need. Vermeer Charitable Foundation has found significance in providing assistance to fill needs of people." The parallels between the Foundation's philosophy and the company's philosophy are apparent.

There are also parallels between Gary's farming interests and his giving instincts. Lois Vermeer, who as the Foundation's executive secretary has to schedule its biannual meetings around planting and harvesting times, readily sees those similarities. After all, when the Foundation funds a scholarship, supports a missionary, or constructs a building, isn't it planting hopes and growing opportunities for people?

To take that analogy further, consider that the doctrine of the Christian Reformed Church of which Gary and Matilda are members emphasizes the importance of people making a difference in God's Kingdom. In that respect, communities worldwide harvest the benefits from the work accomplished by the students, the missionaries, and others supported by the Foundation.

In the initial stages, Ralph strongly influenced charitable giving. Over the years, Matilda has also been a strong influence: "I always say to him, 'You made money, you have to give it away.' And he does."

Always a strong leader in the Foundation, Gary, even today [2008], continues to participate in its meetings. "Gary still chairs the Foundation," said Lois. "He comes to the annual meeting. He calls the annual meeting to order. He still has a voice in the decisions that are made."

In addition to Gary as president of the Foundation board, other board members include Matilda, Bob and Lois Vermeer, Mary and Dale Andringa, and three members of the third generation: Christy Vermeer, Allison Van Wyngarden, and Jason Andringa.

The board makes its funding decisions based on several guidelines. Among them, the board will:

- Give grants only to non-profit organizations—not individuals—primarily in the Pella area and other communities from which Vermeer employees commute.
- Give funding to select mission and educational causes from the Christian Reformed Church and the Reformed Church of America.

In Search of a Better Way
The Lives and Legacies of Gary and Matilda Vermeer
251

For Gary, it is generally important that the Foundation avoid funding an entire project. He believes in a shared responsibility—particularly for community projects. "He favors putting a challenge grant out to grow the community's desire to give," said Lois. "And if that desire wasn't there, then the project wasn't meant to be, in his view."

Just as the company keeps Biblical principles at the center of its philosophy, the Foundation keeps God central in its mission. The Foundation's brochure states, "The Vermeer Charitable Foundation is an agent of God's resources, a witness to God's goodness, and a servant for key projects locally, regionally, and worldwide to ultimately bring honor and praise to God."

The Foundation also references a Bible verse from Paul's second letter to the Corinthians: "Yes, you will be enriched so that you can give even more generously. And when we take your gifts to those who need them, they will break out in thanksgiving to God."[4]

Recipients Over the Years

Practically, this means that the Foundation—one of the top foundations in Iowa in terms of giving[5]—has given away millions for brick and mortar projects, and also has funded specific programs of non-profit groups. Here, in brief, are some of the major recipients or programs of Vermeer and the Vermeer Charitable Foundation:

Scholarships: The Foundation funds scholarship programs at Dordt College in Sioux Center, Iowa; Calvin College and Kuyper College (formerly Reformed Bible College) in Grand Rapids, Michigan; and Fuller Theological Seminary in Pasadena, California. It also funds machine technology and welding scholarships at Indian Hills Community College in Ottumwa, Iowa. In addition, the Foundation annually provides scholarships for up to thirty-five children of Vermeer employees since 1983.

Dordt College: Gary figured prominently in the 1955 founding of Dordt College, which has close ties to the Christian Reformed Church. He served on the college's board of trustees during its formative years, working with Rev. B.J. Haan, the first president, and several other key individuals in getting the college started.[6]

In 1980-81, the Foundation funded the construction of a two-story addition to the science building that houses the engineering department. In 2002, it funded the construction of Dordt's 7,000-square-foot Vermeer Business Center. Among its most notable recent giving was a $350,000 gift announced in 2007 to renovate the school's Science and Technology Center. [7]

"The Vermeer family and Foundation have been a crucial part of Dordt College's development at every stage," said Dr. Carl E. Zylstra, the college's president. "They have always supported the values and convictions of our college."

Central College: Pella's Central College has benefited in many ways from the generosity of the Foundation. Perhaps the Foundation's most notable gift was the Vermeer Science Building, built on Central's campus in the late 1970s.

"When I talked to Gary about naming the building after him, he wasn't interested in doing that," recalled former Central College President Ken Weller. Yet with the size of the donation the Foundation made, Ken thought it would be only appropriate to name the building after him. "But he said 'no.' He didn't believe in self-promotion." After giving it more thought, Ken went back to Gary with the idea of naming the building after Gary's great-grandfather, Brant Vermeer. Gary agreed.

A plaque at the building explains the honor given to Brant Vermeer, who "provided outstanding leadership for early colonists. Throughout subsequent years, his descendants have distinguished themselves in serving this community in the areas of agriculture, industry, education, finance, government, medicine and religion."

Gary and Matilda, personally and through the Foundation, provided funding to Calvin College and many other educational and religious institutions.

Calvin College: This CRC-affiliated college in Grand Rapids, Michigan, has educated several of Gary and Matilda's children and grandchildren. Among the Foundation's gifts to this school is funding for the Vermeer Engineering Projects Center.

Help for Other Non-profits: Terry Butler, Vermeer Corporation's director of environmental, health, safety, and mission support, has traveled the world helping the strategic planning efforts of non-profit organizations such as the Association of Evangelical and Development Relief Organizations, Partners Worldwide, and Serve Our Youth. The Foundation funds this planning.

Disaster relief: The company and its dealers provide disaster-relief services to communities in need. They donated the use of tree spades in 1983 to transplant trees threatened by a road-widening project at the Iowa State Fairgrounds. They donated the use of equipment to plant trees at the memorial for victims of the Oklahoma City bombing. They donated equipment and supported volunteers

Vermeer employees and equipment helped with the cleanup after a tornado devastated Greensburg, Kansas, in 2007.

to help clean up after a tornado hit Oklahoma in 1997. The company and employees also helped more recently in southern coastal areas that were hit by Hurricane Katrina in 2005; in Greensburg, Kansas, a town destroyed by a 2007 tornado; and in several communities in Iowa that were hit early in 2007 by an ice storm. The Foundation and Vermeer pick up the tab for these relief services.

When the company gets involved in a large-scale relief effort, it frequently works with an organization founded by Franklin Graham called Samaritan's Purse, which trains relief workers to provide sensitive and compassionate relief efforts, said Terry Butler, who coordinates the company's response. On smaller-scale and more local relief efforts, the company coordinates its work directly with a community's local officials. The Foundation supports Vermeer employees who volunteer to help and also provides tools and other equipment they need, such as chain saws, rakes, hard hats, ear protection, and more.

Vermeer Cares: The Foundation works with Vermeer employees to help coworkers in need or in crisis. For example, when an employee experienced a devastating house fire, other employees donated money and vacation time to allow that employee the opportunity to deal with the upheaval the fire caused, while the Foundation covered the costs associated with the demolition of the house. Another project of Vermeer Cares is the military care package project in which employees and the Foundation donate items to give to employees' family members in the military.

Pella Christian High School: To replace its aging school, Pella Christian High School supporters launched a successful $20 million fund drive, and opened a new school early in 2008 on the southeast outskirts of Pella.

The Foundation—as well as Gary and Matilda and other family members personally—has been a major contributor to this school, from which all three members of the second generation and all eight of the third generation graduated.

The Vermeer family and the Vermeer Charitable Foundation were among the donors contributing to the new facilities for Pella Christian High School, which opened in 2008.

The school represented a project that Gary felt strongly about. "We made a nice donation to the Christian high school," Gary said in September 2007. "We went to look at it, and boy, that is a beautiful building." His example isn't lost on his family.

"He's a very generous person, and he does enjoy giving back to the community," said Granddaughter Mindi Vanden Bosch. "I think he's a good role model."

The Foundation's high school gift as well as the funds given for building projects at several colleges support Gary's long-standing penchant for brick and mortar projects. The second generation encouraged the Foundation to support scholarships and help the company's own employees. Now, with the addition of the third generation at the table, environmental programs are being discussed. For instance, the Foundation recently gave a grant to the Nature Conservancy, a conservation organization that works around the world to protect ecologically important lands and waters.

Although the second and third generations consider a wider variety of projects, their focus remains consistent with the priorities Gary has shown in his life. Perhaps providing scholarships is the second-generation's way of living Gary's legacy of providing opportunities for people. Perhaps the third-generation's concern about the environment developed as they observed their grandfather's love for his land and its animals.

A complete list of Foundation-supported projects over the years is too lengthy to include here, and to give a partial list would unfairly represent the extent of the Foundation's reach and the recipient organizations themselves.

Naturally, because the Foundation's focus is so intertwined with the faith of its founders, it provides funding to many national and worldwide missions and missionaries. In addition, it has supported many schools, primarily private Christian schools and colleges, particularly in Iowa, but also throughout the country. A great many churches, too, have benefited from the support they've received from the Foundation. This includes Christian churches of many denominations, from Baptist, Catholic, Reformed, Christian Reformed, and many others in the Pella area of which Vermeer employees are members.

In addition to those projects that clearly carry a faith focus, the Foundation supports other area non-profit organizations and projects, often giving preference to those brought to its attention by a Vermeer employee. These include not just organizations who serve disadvantaged people, but also organizations that support historical, sporting, and theatrical projects, for instance.

Back to the Heart: The Roots of a Giving Spirit

What spurred Gary and Matilda's interest in the community, their support for brick and mortar projects, and other projects throughout the world? Certainly, part of the answer lies in their upbringing.

Gary, along with his brothers Dutch, John, and Harry, were raised foremost as sons of an Iowa farmer. They all did their share of milking, spreading manure, hoeing button weeds, and shocking oats.

But they were also raised as the sons of Jacob and Anna, both of whom knew the value of community involvement. Anna was the daughter of a prominent architect and contractor active in his hometown of Grand Rapids, Michigan. Jacob, who obtained a correspondence degree in law, was a member and leader of many boards and organizations in the Pella area.

As such, the boys came to assume without giving it much thought that they, too, would become active in their community. And all four of them were— extraordinarily so. Dutch, a World War II veteran who landed on Normandy Beach on D-Day, served many years in the state legislature and as assistant to Iowa Governor Robert Ray. John led statewide organizations devoted to his interest in horticulture, and was active on several boards. Harry became CEO of a local bank after he left Vermeer, and he, too, served on many local boards and established his own foundation.

Meanwhile, Matilda was raised by a particularly benevolent father who, though he never had much, was apt to generously share what he had. His example, combined with the frugal lifestyle in which she was raised, has been reinforced by her strong faith and her naturally kind heart. So, she too, grew to become both interested and obliged to help her community however she could.

Hospital Fund Drives—With Flair

One of Gary's first community-wide projects came about in 1958, when the city put together an investigating committee to assess community support to build a hospital in Pella. Until this time, the nearest hospital was in Oskaloosa, about twenty miles down the road. Several previous attempts to raise funds for a Pella hospital had failed.

A 1958 article in the Pella Chronicle *announced the exciting news that the community raised enough funds to build the hospital. Gary, on the ladder, unveiled the grand total after lengthening the thermometer.*

Gary and Stu Kuyper, whose family owned Pella Corporation, headed this effort, probably the first of several times that these two industrialists coordinated their efforts for the good of the community. Others who joined the project from the beginning included community leaders such as Max Hoeksema, Henry Klein, Verle Ver Dught, JB Dahm, Henry Vande Voort, Bert Boat, and John Van Dyk.[8] A month later, a Women's Advisory Committee was appointed, led by Martha Lautenbach.[9]

The community obtained federal funding authorized by the Hill-Burton Act, which funded a major part of the construction. The committee was charged with raising the remaining $450,000 necessary to build the Pella hospital.

On May 22, 1958, the fund drive began.[10] It turned out that Gary ran fund drives like his conversations.

"The whole drive took only four weeks," said Max Hoeksema. "That's how Gary operated, you know."

"Gary was a key person for getting a hospital in Pella," said Bob Dieleman, a Pella native and former Vermeer employee. "He went back and forth among some of the money people in Pella. If there was one key individual in getting the hospital here, it was Gary."

Gary seemed to make use of all the tools he had in his arsenal to raise those funds—a little bit of showmanship and plenty of persuasive tactics and hard work. Gary put in $25,000 to launch the effort; Stu Kuyper put in $50,000.

At first, it seemed that the community wasn't going to support the project. "None of us really wanted to do this, but we decided that we would sell memorials—$5,000 to fund a room, lesser amounts to fund smaller items like wheelchairs," said Max Hoeksema. "It was the only way we were going to accomplish our job."

"We talked people into giving $3,000 and got a lot of people to do it," said Gary. "Max Hoeksema and I would work on them."

According to local legend, sometime during this drive or a later drive, Gary called on someone he thought had sufficient resources for a significant contribution. Gary challenged him to give a responsible amount. The man, however, hesitated. He had to give to his struggling Roman Catholic church.

"Maybe you should consider the broader possibilities for giving than just to your church," Gary told him.

The man protested. "You Protestants wouldn't give to the Catholic church."

Whereupon Gary pulled out his checkbook and asked, "How much do you want?" The man was stunned: Gary was willing to match the man's contribution to the hospital with his own contribution to the Catholic church.

A thermometer hanging on the outside of Marion County Bank in downtown Pella charted the fund drive's progress. Every Saturday night, firefighters rolled a fire truck next to the bank and raised the ladder so that Gary could climb up to reach the thermometer and revise the fundraising totals.

In the end, the fund drive was more successful than anyone had hoped. The committee had a date set for the grand finale—when they planned to announce the grand total. As that date neared, it became clear to those closely involved that they would exceed their goal, though they had no idea by how much. That put them in a bit of a predicament. They didn't want to be forced to announce they had met their goal before the grand finale event. Nor did they want to cut off people who still truly wanted to contribute.

Max takes responsibility for deciding not to push the various fundraising committees to report their totals as speedily as he would have otherwise. Nor did he push the recorder to record as quickly as she might have. "We wanted to be fair," said Max. "We wanted everyone to have an equal chance to be part of it, to contribute."

Finally, the night of the grand finale arrived. About 1,000 people gathered downtown that Saturday to hear the announcement. Fire engines with sirens blaring came from all four directions to converge on the bank corner. The city band marched "to a brisk cadence" and when the band played, "the streets echoed with some of the most spirited march music heard since Barnum & Bailey's Circus Band last paraded the town," according to the local newspaper, the *Pella Chronicle*. The newspaper went on to give a detailed account of what happened next:

> The thermometer was resting at $426,000 when Gary Vermeer climbed the ladder to make the final register. As usual, Finance Chairman Max Hoeksema searched the long roll of adding machine tape to find the totals and relate them to Vermeer. A loud ovation was heard when the goal-sum of $450,000 was announced and registered, but the amount of pledges continued to climb. The half-million mark was reached—as high as the thermometer could go. Loud cheers rang out from the crowd. But when it was reported an extension would be added, a hush came over the crowd.

After the extension was added, Gary was to reveal the grand total by flipping over cards that covered the figures at the top of the extension. He started flipping from right to the left.

> There was an atmosphere of suspense as Vermeer slowly turned the cards. When the last one was turned and the unbelievable sum of $630,408.14 was disclosed, a tremendous applause and cheer filled the air.[11]

Gary had led the committee to raise $180,000 more than what was needed for the hospital. The hospital opened December 27, 1960.

"A year later, we started building the nursing home [with the extra money]," Gary said.

The Pella Chronicle *noted how Gary landed his helicopter on top of the Tulip Toren in downtown Pella during a drive to raise funds to expand the Pella hospital.*

Two decades later, when the community launched another fundraiser to expand and update the hospital, Gary again led the fund drive and again turned to showmanship to help raise excitement.

This time, Gary had a platform built at the very top of Pella's Tulip Toren—a 65-foot-tall landmark in downtown Pella's Central Park. There, once a week, he landed his helicopter and someone—sometimes John M. Vos, who headed the Vermeer construction crew, or Arvin Vander Wilt, another crew member, or one of several others—were lowered down in a chair lift by a cable winch. Thus lowered, they marked in red the new fundraising totals on two thermometers erected along the south side of the tower. Crowds gathered each week on Franklin Street to watch.

This time the goal was $3 million. Twenty-five donors had put up a $1.5 million challenge grant; the Pella community was asked to contribute the remaining $1.5 million.

Again, Gary used a variety of persuasive tactics to encourage donations. He hired Ken Weller, then a fairly new president of Central College, as a consultant for the factory and family with the understanding that Ken would donate his consulting fees to the drive.

About that same time, Dealer Kevin Klein was working as a regional sales representative for Vermeer, a job that frequently put him out in the field. But it was on one of his days in the office that he was asked to contribute:

"One day, Gary walked in and said, 'Have you ever been in a helicopter before?' I said, 'No,' and he said, 'Follow me.' I had to trot to keep up with his walk. . . . He gets me airborne and he looks at me and says 'Have you made your pledge to the hospital drive?' I say, 'No, but if you promise to get me down safely, I promise I will.' He laughed so hard, I didn't think he would be able to fly the helicopter."

Although Gary initially was skeptical they could raise $3 million in the community, the goal was met. The helicopter landing on a platform, sixty-five feet up, in downtown Pella was the talked-about event of the year—and a long-lasting memory for many local residents even now. At the time, Gary himself realized and took pleasure in the oddity of the event.

"I've been informed by at least a dozen very reliable sources that we had been fined by the FAA all the way from $100 to $27,000 for landing the helicopter on the Tulip Tower," Gary said during the drive's finale event. "Now this is a good story, but it isn't true. In fact, we checked all the regulations for helicopter flying before we did this and could find no regulation that would prohibit such flying."[12]

Dispatching Construction Crews

For decades, Vermeer has had a construction crew on its payroll. The crew has helped build many of the company's buildings, and has worked on other construction and maintenance projects around the plants. One sometimes might wonder, however, how much time this crew had for factory projects given the extent to which Gary loaned it out. He freely lent the crew to projects he believed in and wanted built—a church, a swimming pool, and a restaurant and roller rink, for instance, not to mention various farm and family projects.

In the mid-1970s, the crew worked on Pella's Faith Christian Reformed Church. Gary and Matilda had been members of Calvary Christian Reformed Church, but when the congregation outgrew its building, the couple lent their support to begin a daughter church. "Gary had so much fun starting churches, he wanted to be part of it as well," said Bob Dieleman, also a founding member.

In 1976, the Vermeer construction crew was dispatched, under John M. Vos's capable leadership, to build the Hilltop North addition. Built in 1970, largely with Foundation funding, Hilltop provided much-needed living facilities for Pella's senior generation.

"It came about because we had money from baler royalties," said Gary. "We had several million in the Foundation and thought we should do something with it. The hospital wanted to build it but didn't have funds."

In 1977, Vermeer construction crews built the Pella indoor swimming pool. A couple years earlier, Pella voters had turned down a bond issue to fund the pool. Gary decided to build it anyway. Company crews built the project, and the Vermeer Charitable Foundation donated it to the city. The twenty-five-meter, six-lane pool, with a diving area, opened in September 1977.[13]

During construction, Gary stopped by two or three times a week to check on progress, recalled Arvin Vander Wilt, a member of the construction crew. "Construction was a real important part to Gary Vermeer. He had a lot of ideas of how to proceed with it."

Arvin's paycheck always came through Vermeer Manufacturing Company, though he was well aware that his work often didn't directly benefit the business. "At that time, we all knew it eventually came out of one account anyway: It was Gary Vermeer's bank account that paid us."

Building Recreational Opportunities

Gary's interest in his community included a conviction that it needed to provide recreational opportunities for its residents. Perhaps this belief stemmed from his own restlessness that kept him and his family on the go.

"When I was in junior high, we went to the Newton roller rink a lot," said Daughter Mary, referring to a rink in Newton, nearly thirty miles north. "We also went to the Maple Buffet in Knoxville [about fifteen miles to the southwest]. My dad thought we ought to have those two things in Pella."

Pella's Dutch Buffet and roller rink opened in 1964, a couple of miles east of Pella.

As a result, Pella's all-you-can-eat Dutch Buffet and roller rink opened in 1964, a couple miles east of Pella along what is now known as Old Highway 163.

Characteristically, Gary described his involvement in the project matter-of-factly. "We got a bunch of guys together and put some money in it and built it."

Matilda recalls that she had looked at the project more practically. "I said to Gary, 'What will you do if it folds up?' and Gary said, 'I think we will put corn in it.' I remember that so well. And look how many years they stayed open!"[14]

"A lot of it was Dad's desire to have things for people to do so they could stay in Pella," said Mary. "Dad was intent on adding a lot of value for young people. It opened when I was a freshman in high school. I was one of the waitresses."

The buffet cost two dollars and besides offering employment to many local youth as it did Mary, it also provided Pella another place to eat, while the roller rink hosted high school and youth group skating parties. Mary skated a couple times a month. Gary and Matilda skated, too. They particularly enjoyed the "Grand March" and the special moonlight skating.

A few years later, a ten-lane bowling alley and The Blue Room, a small sandwich shop, were added.

Another recreational pursuit that Gary helped create was the Holland Theatre. He and a group of investors agreed, in the early 1960s, to put up the funds to provide a better place for Central College students, in particular, to watch movies. Pella had one theater, in poor shape, at the time. Vermeer construction crews went to work putting an addition onto an historic building northwest of the downtown square.

Gary's decision to invest, however, didn't sit well with conservative church leaders at the time.[15] "Gary was not overly swayed by public opinion," said his son, Stan. "If he felt it was right, he was going to do it."

The criticism, though, eventually led Gary to donate his stock to Central College, and other investors followed suit. The college owned the theater for

In Search of a Better Way
The Lives and Legacies of Gary and Matilda Vermeer
267

many years before selling it. The theater closed in 2002 when a triplex theater opened in Pella's new Molengracht development.

Mary was in eighth grade when *The Sound of Music* came out. "I went to it with my folks half a dozen times. That might have been the impetus for Dad to realize that a theater with good movies would be good for Pella."

Loyalty to Their Religious Roots

Another major beneficiary was Pella's First Christian Reformed Church (CRC). In 1998, church members became divided on theological issues, and some decided to leave their affiliation with the Christian Reformed denomination. As a result, ownership of the local building came into question.

Gary and Matilda were no longer members of First CRC, but they felt a certain loyalty and benevolence to the congregation. They had both grown up in that church, as had their parents and earlier ancestors. Inside its walls Matilda had first caught Gary's eye. They also remained loyal to their denomination.

As a result, in 1998 they offered the First CRC a donation of one million dollars. As part of an agreement that allowed the congregation to retain both the name and building, First CRC then gave a portion of that money to the group who had chosen to leave the denomination.

Beyond Financing

Although Gary and Matilda's financial contributions to their community, their church, and their world were significant, their community involvement went much deeper.

Gary could have just written a check to the hospital and made a few calls to wealthy Pella residents, but he flew his helicopter weekly to the center of Pella to create a spectacle and generate excitement. Gary and Matilda could have been satisfied with just family time in Canada, but instead generously treated hundreds of people to fishing trips in the wilderness and to water skiing experiences on their lake near Pella.

Gary's contributions also included service on many boards. He served on the consistory, the governing board, for his church. He served as board president and board member for the Pella hospital for years. He also served on boards for the local Christian elementary and high schools, for Dordt College, Pine Rest Christian Hospital, the Pella Chamber of Commerce, Norwest Bank in Des Moines, the Iowa Natural Heritage Foundation, and the Pella airport.

Gary and Matilda's community commitment is illustrated in a story told by Art Ruiter, who in 1985 was director of Pella's Christian Opportunity Center. COC, as it is known locally, started in 1969 to provide classroom space for five children with disabilities. Today, it serves more than 250 people with disabilities, mostly providing adults with residential and vocational services.

Sometime in the winter or early spring of 1985, Gary was hospitalized in Des Moines due to back pain. Later, at home recuperating, Gary, and Matilda, herself down with the flu, watched a TV program that piqued their interest. The show was about wishes granted to children who suffered from terminal illnesses. Perhaps it was their own temporary disabilities at the time or some other reason, but the show got them thinking about the COC clients who suffer from incurable disabilities and who rarely have their special wishes granted.

As soon as he became more mobile, Gary called the COC director.

"Hi, Art, this is Gary. I need to talk to you. When can I see you?"

Within twenty minutes, Gary was at Art's office. He told Art about the TV program, and got to the point immediately. "Matilda and I would like to pay for a trip for the COC clients. We want you to personally take them to Florida or California, to Disneyland and Sea World—some of the places that other people get a chance to visit. We want you to take care of all the arrangements. We'll pay for their travel, food, and motel, and everything."

Momentarily, Art was speechless.

Gary asked, "Do you think this is crazy?"

"Yes, it's crazy—a good kind of crazy! But, Gary, this will cost a lot," Art cautioned.

"We don't care about the cost. Just make the arrangements, and call Matilda when you need money."

Art immediately saw the potential for training for his clients, teaching them how to handle money, how to prepare for a trip, and how to travel. He also knew that he would need quite a few staff members to help with the clients, a fact that surprised Gary who had initially thought that Art and just a couple staff members could easily chaperone the clients.

Art agreed the trip would be a great opportunity for the clients. Then he presented a challenge. "You and Matilda have to go along. You're giving the gift; you need to experience your gift at work"

That startled Gary. It wasn't what he expected. He told Art that he would have to talk it over with Matilda.

Later, when Art and Gary talked again, Gary told Art that he and Matilda accepted the challenge. "Yes, we will go along with you, but only if you treat us as staff members." That was fine with Art, who knew he needed plenty of staff to help with the clients. He told Gary that he had lined up three staff members and eleven clients to make the trip.

Gary and Matilda took a group of clients from Pella's Christian Opportunity Center to Disney World in 1985. This photo appeared in the Pella Chronicle *in June 1985.*

That wasn't what Gary wanted. "You don't understand," Gary told Art. "I'm not talking about a few people. Take all the people who come to COC."

In the end, forty-nine COC clients and eleven staff members, accompanied by Gary and Matilda, went to Florida in May 1985, where they visited Disney World, Epcot, and Sea World. Gary was assigned to drive a van and be the companion for a seventeen-year-old boy who had cerebral palsy. Matilda accompanied a middle-aged female client. They pushed wheelchairs, assisted with the various rides, and helped transport and feed the clients.

When an airline strike forced the group to stay in Florida an extra day and sent Art scrambling to find hotel

In Search of a Better Way
The Lives and Legacies of Gary and Matilda Vermeer
271

accommodations, Gary and Matilda didn't blink at the extra cost. Meanwhile, COC students and some clients whose disabilities precluded them from making the trip were treated by the Vermeers to a day at Adventureland, an amusement park in Des Moines. Adult clients who couldn't make the trip or go to Adventureland were later treated to a day of boating and helicopter rides at Gary's camp near Pella.

For Art as well as the clients, the trip was unforgettable. Gary and Matilda must have thought so, too. "After the trip, I went to the factory and several people stopped me to tell me that Gary had never talked about any other trip as much as he talked about this trip," Art said.

"It was so cool that they were willing to participate," Art added. "I wanted them to be with the people who were disabled, to understand their special needs, and to experience what their gift meant to each of the people served at COC."

When asked for help, some people give their money. Others give their time. Gary and Matilda gave both.

*Matilda dyed Gary's hair in 1997 when they dressed
as farmers for Faith Church's all-church supper to kick
off the fall start of the Sunday School season.*

10 Values of a Lifetime

There is coming a day
When no heartaches shall come,
Nor more clouds in the sky,
No more tears to dim the eye.
All is peace forevermore
On that happy golden shore.
What a day, glorious day that will be.

What a day that will be when my Jesus I shall see
And I look upon his face,
The One who saved me by His grace;
When He takes me by the hand
And leads me through the Promised Land,
What a day, glorious day that will be.

~ From one of Matilda's favorite hymns, "What a Day That Will Be"[1]

When Matilda heard Larry Eggink sing "What a Day That Will Be" at Charles Fopma's funeral, it touched her heart. She told Gary so as they were leaving the service. "I said, after you hear that, you are just ready to go, but Gary said he was not ready for me to go yet."

One of Matilda's favorite Bible verses also talks about meeting Jesus. At the beginning of chapter 14 in the gospel of John, Jesus reassures his disciples:

> Do not let your hearts be troubled. Trust in God; trust also in me. In my Father's house are many rooms; if it were not so, I would have told you. I am going there to prepare a place for you. And if I go and prepare a place for you, I will come back and take you to be with me that you also may be where I am. You know the way to the place where I am going.

"That is a real comfort, I think," said Matilda. "It is something to look forward to. I can't imagine the mansions. If you really think what heaven will be like, you can't understand it."

Raised during the depression in a small, conservative, and religious town in the heart of farm country, Matilda and Gary made an impact on thousands. Today, we see their influence in the Vermeer machines at the job sites, in the brick and mortar projects filled with college students, and in pictures in photo albums across the country of grinning people holding a prized fish in Canada.

The Vermeers didn't need to do what they have done. They could have built the company and lived a life of leisure as many wealthy Americans have. What made them different? Why bother to get so involved?

For instance, why did Matilda, with her own three young children finally out of diapers, voluntarily take in an infant for eleven months, an infant whom she knew she couldn't keep?

And, why did Gary—a man who has had a lifelong distaste for debt—once borrow money in order to give it away?

And why do Gary and Matilda—who have a net worth in the millions—live in a fifty-five-year-old house worth less than $100,000?

Those answers lie in their values.

Faith

A discussion of Gary and Matilda's values must begin with their faith in God. The couple incorporates—and openly shares—their faith in their daily lives. Although not overt in her faith, Matilda quietly lives and shares her faith in a way that is unmistakable.

Matilda demonstrates her faith in quiet ways.

As a youth, she thought she wanted to grow up to work in an orphanage. As Matilda grew into adulthood, she devoted hours helping with various church projects, from teaching Sunday School and Vacation Bible School to helping various women's groups such as the Ladies Aid or the Lydia Society. She painted parking lot markings during a mission trip to the Rehoboth Christian School, a school founded by the Christian Reformed Church near Gallup, New Mexico, where most students are Native American, Hispanic, or members of other ethnic minorities.[2]

Matilda also has hosted missionaries in her home for years. "It's not like she had a great house for hosting, but she was a gracious hostess," said Mary Andringa. "I think the missionaries would often stay over a weekend, to speak at church events."

Mary, who once entertained a notion of becoming a missionary herself, remembers Dr. Peter and Eleanor Boelens and Michiel and Trudy De Berdt talking about their experiences around her mother's kitchen table. "It intrigued me a lot."

Besides her involvement with missions, Matilda also demonstrated her faith in quieter ways with those she came in contact.

For example, Matilda regularly visited people in the hospital and nursing homes, providing comfort not just to the person she visited but quite often to their families as well:

In the spring of 2004, Dick Gabrielse called his mother's room at the Pella Nursing Home. Matilda answered the phone. Dick knew Matilda, and knew that she frequently visited his mother, Annetta, then well into her nineties and suffering from poor health. Dick told Matilda that his brother had just passed away, and that he was en route to Pella to break the news to his mother.

"We'll be here waiting for you," Matilda told Dick on the phone. Dick, still at least four hours away from Pella, told her that he appreciated her gesture but that it wasn't necessary for her to stay that long with his mother. "We'll be here," Matilda repeated. "I want to do that, and Gary will be here, too."

When Dick arrived, together they told his mother about her son's death. Dick has never forgotten Matilda's compassion that day. "It was just a precious experience because she was so caring. She is like an angel."

That comparison has been used by others as well.

"Matilda changed my life in a religious way because of her belief in God," said Jerry Lundy, who owned the camp in Canada many of the years that Gary and Matilda vacationed there. Jerry got to know Matilda better while Gary escorted guests on his floatplane for a day of fishing at a remote lake. "Matilda stayed in camp, and I would go and chitchat with her. I never met anyone in my life as close to an angel as she was.

"She was so true. She was so sincere and honest. I never have seen another person like that, ever."

Matilda's compassion and flexibility complemented and smoothed out Gary's personality, who in his own way demonstrated similar values.

Providing Growth Opportunities

In 1969, Art Swank was managing a Vermeer-owned dealership in New Jersey when he was offered a sales position with a dealership in the Kansas City area owned by Doug Wilson and Henry Monster. The offer included the opportunity to buy half the dealership within five years. Art jumped at the chance, but it wasn't until after he had made the move that he learned that there was yet another hurdle in the deal: he would need the approval of Vermeer Manufacturing Company to enter into an ownership agreement with Doug and Henry.

As it turned out, five years later Art was given the chance to buy the entire dealership. But obtaining the OK from Harry Vermeer, Carl Boat, and Gary was a challenge he had to surmount.

"I had apparently ruffled some feathers with Carl and Harry and needed to travel to Pella and plead my case in front of all of them," Art recalled. "During this way-too-long meeting, Gary didn't say much until they were going to make the decision. Gary said, 'The question comes down to: Is Art honest? Can Art sell? Does he have the financial ability to do this? If all these questions are answered yes, then we need to give the kid a chance.'

I have been a dealer for thirty-seven years because Gary gave me a chance."

Gary never was overly concerned about credentials. He didn't particularly care what education people had. He often has noted that Arnie Mathes, whom he considered one of the company's best engineers, had only a sixth-grade education. Nor did he care where people were on the social ladder.

"When I went back to those year-end (dealer) meetings, Gary would come by to shake my hand," said Kevin Klein, a Lincoln, Nebraska, dealer. "Even though I was one of his smaller dealers, he never made me feel small. He always made me feel good about who I was."

"When people knew Gary [as a successful businessman] they had him on this pedestal," said Arlene Thomassen, who worked with Gary on various church projects. "I never had that sense with Gary because I had worked at a table with him head to head. He recognized talent from the lowliest of people. He didn't belittle and he was not a BS-er, just a good business man."

What was important to Gary was effort. "If you want to put forth the effort, there's a lot of opportunity to advance in this company," Gary has said.

That's true, agreed Dealer Denny Vander Molen. "Gary was a tremendously driven guy who was very engaged in what was going on with the product. If you could hang with him with the work ethic, you were going to do all right with Gary," said Denny, whose dealership now includes seven locations covering customers in Tennessee, Mississippi, Arkansas, and Louisiana.

"Some of the people he put in management positions in stores throughout the country were people you would never expect," said Bob Dieleman, who knew Gary both because of his own association with Vermeer and through their church. "He recognized something in them; they would do what he said, and became quite wealthy. He recognized what type of people worked well for him."

John Vos was a rambunctious kid right out of high school when Vermeer hired him as a factory demonstrator. His dad, John M. Vos, had been head of Gary's construction crew for many years, which John acknowledges probably helped him get the job. "The job was traveling around the country, and that's all I really wanted to know. Gary trained me on a tree remover, the first product I demonstrated."

John's career grew from that factory demonstrator into a dealer with eight locations on the East Coast. Gary, Harry, Carl Boat, and others "gave me opportunities in life that I could never really thank them properly for," John said.

Providing Employment Opportunities

Gary's lack of concern about a person's education or social status extended in several directions. As early as the 1950s, Vermeer was employing people with disabilities, a practice that has continued.

"It's nice if they've got something to do," Gary has said, "and they generally can make their way."

Gary also commonly dropped the names of farmers who needed jobs—both seasonally or cyclically during bad farming years and encouraged his managers to hire them. Gary believed farmers were especially good workers.

A good worker with a lack of education? Sure, Gary would say, hire him. Disabled? Sure, no problem. Farmers in need of work? Definitely. Refugees? Okay, that, too. Over the years, he is known to have specifically agreed to the hiring of refugees from Southeast Asia and Cuba.

And during slow times at the factory, especially early on, Gary did what he could to keep his employees working. "We tried to work as the orders dictated," said Keith Nibbelink, who started at the factory in 1954. "If we had a lot of orders, we worked long hours, sixty or so hours a week. Other times, things were slow, and they cut us back to thirty-two hours a week." During these times, Gary invited his employees to hoe or pick tomatoes that he had planted on a farm north of town. "He tried to keep us all busy. He had the good of his employees at heart."

Focus on Youth

People who came to know Gary in his older years describe him as a no-nonsense person chiefly concerned with matters of importance to him: the factory, farming, hunting, and fishing. Working with teenagers probably isn't a job they associate with Gary. And for some people, thinking of teenagers flocking to Gary requires a stretch of the imagination.

Yet that's what happened.

In the Christian Reformed Church in past decades, Young People's Society—a group for teenagers—met once a week and generally included time for both Bible study and socializing. Perhaps once a month, the group held a larger social, such as ice skating or roller skating.

Gary led this group, first at the First Christian Reformed Church in Pella and then later at Calvary Christian Reformed Church.

Teens from other churches came to their Young People's Society because Gary was such a talented leader and they had such great socials, said Keith Nibbelink, who belonged to the group at First CRC. "He could relate to young people really well. He had an open mind, and we would discuss anything we wanted to. He would either agree or show us why he didn't agree."

"He was really good with the Bible studies," said Marsha Overbergen, a cousin fourteen years his junior. "He was so knowledgeable. He had a good way of bringing it out—putting it down to earth to our daily living so that we wanted to live that way and be that way."

At First CRC, Gary encouraged the teens to formally debate topics such as reconciling free will with predestination. Gary flew the winning team members to eat at the Cloud Room, a nice restaurant at the Des Moines airport, often challenging them to try the frog legs on the menu. Later, he typically flew the losing team, too.

While at Calvary Christian Reformed Church, Gary sometimes led a discussion about current topics that followed the hour-long Bible study. He set up incentives to encourage the teens to contribute to the discussion. Once, he decided the youths should stage their own Kennedy-Nixon debate. Although none of the participants wanted to argue in favor of a Democrat or a Catholic for president, finally Stan De Vries and Bob Dieleman took that side. The youths spent several weeks talking about it, the discussion was so intense. No one switched viewpoints, but the discussion it generated was fun and spirited.

It's no wonder that Gary's Young People's group was thriving and attracted so many young people from other churches.

Yet Gary had another drawing card in his pocket. He directed young people in thirteen plays—plays such as *The Calamity Kids*, and *Cheaper by the Dozen*, and *A Man Called Peter*.

Most of the plays were presented in the Pella Christian High School gymnasium. Some were held in what is now Farver Auditorium in Pella's Community Center. "We had a packed house for two nights at least. We made a lot of money for the group," said Keith Nibbelink. "I'm sure a lot of people look back and think Gary had a good influence on them."

"Gary's directing was somewhat minimal, but he had the ability to pick the right people for the right positions. And then he turned them loose to develop their own part," said Bob Dieleman, a cast member in *The Calamity Kids*.

Gary, dressed for a murder mystery party

Once, the curtain was supposed to have closed on a scene, but someone forgot to pull the rope. The actors started ad-libbing and pulled the curtain shut themselves. "Ad-libbing really tickled Gary," said Bob.

"He was very good at directing the plays. He somehow was very motivational," said Judy VerHeul, who was in Young People's Society before she graduated from high school in 1962. "It was a very positive part of my growing-up years. He enjoyed us, and I think that made it even more special to us."

In addition to directing, Gary took on the role of promoter by establishing incentives for the youths to sell tickets. Sell the most tickets, and win a plane ride to Des Moines to eat at the airport's Cloud Room, he told them. "Needless to say we had sellouts. Plane rides were unique at that time," said Bob Dieleman.

Whether it was for that reason, or as a reward for something else, Judy VerHeul and a friend won one of those plane rides to the Cloud Room. "It was sort of a reward. We all got to do that. I never would have gone to the Cloud Room without going with Gary Vermeer. I think he did nothing but reinforce our worth. It was a positive thing for all of us for him to have given us that attention."

Once the youth had learned the play, Gary believed in putting it on several times. Not only did they perform it in Pella, but they were apt to take it on the road, sometimes just 30 miles down the road to Oskaloosa and sometimes 290 miles northwest to Hull, Iowa, where they performed at Western Christian High School.

Besides the Bible studies, the debates, the plays, and the plane rides, Gary also made sure there were social activities for the youth group. He accompanied youth to Newton to roller skate. He invited them to his cabin on a lake just north of town for a night of water skiing and volleyball. In the winter, he invited them to ice skate on his lake where he had set up lights and served hot chocolate.

Open to New Thinking

There is a story about Gary Vermeer's great grandmother who, when reproached about washing dishes on Sunday, said, *"Alle vuiligheid is geen heiligheid.* [Filthiness is not holiness.]"[3]

Gary had strong opinions. Many think of him as tough-minded and inflexible. But like his great grandmother, Gary also was practical and he could be startlingly open-minded for his age and his conservative, religious roots. That was why he could attract so many youth to his Bible studies.

Even his grandchildren have noticed that he can be open-minded about some issues. "One thing I really value about Grandpa is that he is pretty nonjudgmental, especially when it comes to judging people based on gender, race, or religion. He doesn't pigeonhole people," said Heidi Quist.

Although some in his denomination want to restrict the roles women play, "Grandpa has no problem with that at all," Heidi added. "He'll say Jesus spread his Word through men and women. We felt real support from him—Whoever God makes you to be, be that."

His willingness to accept differing views extended to other denominations as well. "He had clear beliefs himself," Heidi said, but could accept if you weren't part of that particular church. "He had the view that we can't be prideful, that we know who God is."

"Gary was a feminist before his time." said Dale Andringa, his son-in-law. "I never got a sense that he thought his daughter was limited by virtue of her gender. He didn't spend a lot of time encouraging people to do things, he just assumed they would. As a consequence, his daughter and granddaughters were exposed to a view that was very healthy."

"It says a lot about who he is as a father because my Aunt Mary has been given so much opportunity in such a male-dominated environment," added Heidi. "In that respect, he was an empowering father."

"I don't remember him saying you can't do something," agreed Mary. "He was not negative. He was a possibility person. He assumed his kids were going to use their judgment. He thought cheerleading was a silly idea, but once I was a cheerleader, he came to most all of the games. I don't think he would have come otherwise."

Gary's open views also played out in the adult Bible studies in which he took part. Details are sketchy, but Gary evidently took great pleasure in debating theological issues.

"Gary wasn't afraid of controversial topics. He rather relished them," said Harriet Zylstra, one of the members of a couples' Bible study with Gary and Matilda that spanned several decades. "Gary always had lots of leading questions. He loved a good discussion. If it became a little controversial he loved that. He would just sit there and grin."

They studied Genesis one year—talked about the length of days of creation—and studied the books of James and Galatians other years. Once, a Catholic priest met with the group.

Another time, after Rev. Gerald Van Oyen and his wife Ellen left Calvary CRC to move to Michigan, the entire Bible study group decided to visit the Van Oyens for a Sunday evening Bible study. "Some members drove up because they had time to take the whole day," said Harriet. "I was in school, and Gary and Matilda flew Bob [Zylstra] and me for a Bible Study. We just stayed overnight after the Bible Study and flew back."

Gary also had a sense of humor about the church. Harriet recalls a time when the couples were playing cards, Gary and Matilda brought up tongue-in-cheek that playing Hearts violated the church policy of 1928.[4]

Another time, Harriet and Bob Zylstra were traveling in Africa with Gary and Matilda. That was when they created the "First Epistle of VerZyl to the Church of Indecision" that they mailed to the Bible study group back home. "Gary had so much fun writing that letter from VerZyl [a made-up term combining parts of the names *Vermeer* and *Zylstra*]," Harriet said. "His whole body enjoys things. He was always taking off his glasses and rubbing the tears from his eyes with the palms of his hands."

Still later, when Ken Weller, then president of Central College, visited Gary as part of his role of keeping a major donor updated and informed, Gary often brought up theology. Ken was active in the Reformed Church in America, and Gary was interested in what was going on in the denominational level—what the topics of dissension were, for instance, the role of women, or attitude toward missionaries. Gary wanted to learn about them, thinking he might be able to apply their lessons to his own Christian Reformed Church.

Tithes and Offerings

Faith Christian Reformed Church elders, 1968, from left: Lou Van Haaften, Bernie Van Ee, Gary Vermeer, Lou Van Wyk, and John De Nooy

In the Christian Reformed tradition, church elders take part in a practice known in Dutch as *huis bezoek* or house visitation. Traditionally, two elders from the church annually called on each family of the congregation for a formal visit lasting one hour. Although the practice is fading somewhat today and taking different forms, when Stan, Bob, and Mary were growing up, *huis bezoek* was a formal and serious affair, that if truth be known, scared more than one child.

The elders typically asked about the family's spiritual practices, asked the children a few questions about school, and asked if there were any questions or problems the family wanted to discuss.

"At *huis bezoek,* my dad said how important it was to him that we tithe—that we give back to the Lord," said Mary. "That was an unquestioned part of our life."[5]

Stan and Mary remember the Biblical principle of tithing as something they overheard and learned more by observation than by direct instruction. "When I started working at Dutch Buffet, I know I gave money back," said Mary. Bob, however, remembers tithing discussions as more explicit. "I just remember that giving back was something that they instilled in us. They took the Bible verse which talks about tithing, and we discussed it.

"They certainly gave away more than their ten percent," Bob continued. "And we, as their kids, have done that, too. It is commanded in Scripture, and we have followed that. Dad and Mom both believed that if you were blessed, you needed to give back."

Good Marriage

Although both Gary's parents and Matilda's parents stayed together and remained married their entire lives, neither Gary nor Matilda would characterize their parents' marriages as particularly happy.[6] Neither couple was affectionate— neither Gary nor Matilda can remember ever seeing their parents kiss.

Perhaps it was because of the tensions they felt in their own family lives growing up that Gary and Matilda felt strongly about creating a happy and stable marriage for themselves. "We agreed that no matter what happened, we would always try to make the other person happy," Gary said.[7] "Gary always said, 'if you do something to make the other person happy, then you make yourself happy, too,'" said Matilda. "That is so true."[8]

Gary and Matilda enjoy playing cards with family and friends.

In any case, a strong marriage for themselves and seeing their children make strong marriages have been important to the couple.

"Once my dad was asked what his greatest success was and he answered that he had three children with good marriages and grandchildren who have good marriages," said Mary. "Stable families are important to him." And Mary believes that part of Gary's deep inclination to provide activities for his family and community were part of his way of helping to ensure stable families.

Punctuality

If Gary said a meeting would start at 7 a.m., employees knew to count on it. If Gary said his plane would leave Pella at 7 a.m., travelers knew to be there at 6:45 a.m. Gary started early and was always prompt, wherever he was.

"He would get up early in the morning when we were traveling and by the time we got up he already had the whole day arranged," said Harriet Zylstra. "Everything was very much on time. Matilda would caution him a little: 'They are our guests and if they want to sleep a little longer, we need to let them do that, Gary.'

"Don't ever try to call Gary after 8:30 p.m.," Harriet added. "He's in bed. He doesn't like to be disturbed. And he is always prompt."

Gary's inclination for punctuality is well known. "If you were going to go anywhere with Gary, you had better be at least fifteen minutes early," said John Vander Wert, a longtime employee. "That's just the way he was."

Living the Simple Life

To this day, Gary and Matilda live in the small three-bedroom, one-bathroom ranch they built in 1953 just east of the factory campus.[9] It has no basement. An oak and a sycamore dominate the front yard. A room air-conditioning unit juts out from a front window. Mahaska County valued the 1,680-square-foot house at just over $85,530 in 2007.

Including the house, the outbuildings (three barns built in 1910, 1939 and 1940; a 1982 steel utility building and a few other smaller buildings), and 28 acres, the property is valued at $125,950.

Like the exterior, the home's interior is simple and functional. The living room includes a couple recliners and a couch. A picture of a mill by a river hangs on one wall. A Vermeer painting of a maid with a pitcher hangs on another. Family pictures rest on a spinet piano, while another is on the wall above it.

In the entry, a large wooden plaque with a verse from Matthew hangs on the wall. It is a gift handmade by Rev. John Engbers, "Ask and it will be given to you. Seek and you will find. Knock and the door will be opened for you. For every one who asks, receives; he who seeks, finds; and to him who knocks, the door will be opened" Matthew 7: 7 & 8.

Not surprisingly, the Vermeers' attitude toward their home is practical and easygoing.

For example, the couple's kitchen ceiling still sports an old-fashioned circular fluorescent light. The couple never bothered updating the light when they learned it would have required them to repaint the ceiling. When they replaced the kitchen faucet, they initially wanted a single lever, but readily agreed to a two-handled faucet when the store only had that kind in stock.

Gary and Matilda have lived 55 years in their home.

Gary and Matilda raised their three children in that home and babysat their grandchildren in that home. It was the home base from which they traveled from Antarctica to the North Pole, from Africa to Australia, and most points in between. It is in that house that Gary authorized checks worth millions of dollars to benefit the Pella community as well as religious and educational institutions around the country.

Their lifestyle, too, generally has remained simple. Matilda hates shopping for clothes, said her daughter-in-law Alma. She believes in buying local whenever possible, and buys most of her clothes at Mode Huis, a store that operated for many years in Pella but has since moved to Newton. That's where family members turn to buy Matilda Christmas presents.

"Matilda will never, in any way, shape, or form, let you believe she has a penny," said Jerry Lundy, the Canadian camp operator. "She is uncomfortable with wealth. She is quite happy with plain clothes."

The same goes for Gary. "Gary will not do any bragging. He won't go there. That is the beauty of Gary. The bragging never comes through," says Arlene Thomassen, who knew Gary from church.

"I never had a sense he was doing it to make all this money," Arlene added. "He was just doing it because he could do it. Therein lie his humility and his Christianity. All his philanthropy and giving really come from the right place."

Gary's expenditures tend to be practical, and when they aren't, then they are to provide opportunity. Although he readily spent money to travel, he wouldn't think of staying at a Hilton if there was a Super 8 available. "Even though he had fun, he still wanted to be economical. He liked the latest radar on his planes. He bought a helicopter. But a five-course dinner at a luxury hotel was not of any interest to him," said Bob Vermeer.

Gary and Matilda's simple lifestyle is a fact that hasn't been lost on Vermeer employees over the years. It is more common than not for employees to take dealers, their customers, and even their own families, on a drive past the modest home of the company founder. The irony never fails to astonish.

Gary and Matilda never needed fancy restaurants. McDonald's is one of Gary's favorites.

"Gary is a very common individual. Some people had a hard time realizing that," said longtime employee John Vander Wert. "The Vermeers continued to live in their little three-bedroom house. We would point out that's where Mr. Vermeer lives, and many people had a hard time with that."

And more than one visitor to the plant has been surprised to discover that the plain-spoken man in overalls they've been talking to was the company founder.

John recalled a particular annual meeting with dealers when Gary encouraged his dealers to cut back. Many of them were buying houses and boats despite an economic downturn at the time. "'Things are getting tough; you'd better cut down,' Gary advised the dealers that year. 'My wife just got an automatic clothes washer, and she doesn't even have a dishwasher.'

"There was no putting on a big front with Gary," said John.

Despite the successful factory, the world travels, the generous philanthropy, and the resulting attention and fame that must have brought its own temptations—the couple remains rooted in their values.

And when directly asked what lesson they would most like to pass on to their children, the couple turns to their values to find the answer.

"To have a good marriage," Gary answered.

"To be kind to each other, and to not live for yourself, but live for the glory of God," Matilda added.

"God blesses us, and all that we are is a gift from God," said Matilda. "I know Gary has made a world of money and all that, but it's God who made who we are. All the praise is truly for the glory of God."

Amen.

Source Notes*

1 Beginnings

1   Gary Vermeer, speech at Customer Day, July 21, 1997.
2   Stan Vermeer, interview with Making History, April 16, 1998. Making History is a company Vermeer Corporation hired to research its history and provide relevant information to create the exhibits in the Vermeer Museum.
3   Arnold B. Skromme, The 7-Ability Plan, The Self-Confidence Press, Moline, Illinois, 1989, p. 12.
4   Gary Vermeer, speech to Antique Tractor Club, March 21, 1997.
5   Ibid.
6   Skromme, p. 14.
7   Gary Vermeer, speech to Antique Tractor Club, March 21, 1997.
8   Gary Vermeer, transcript of interview by Lee Klyn, WHO Radio, Des Moines.
9   Ibid.
10 "Here's where Vermeer Began," Pow-R-Line, a Vermeer publication.
12 Ibid.
13 Gary Vermeer, interview by Klyn.
4   Case Vander Hart, interview with Making History, March 31, 1998.
5   Arlie Vander Hoek, interview with Making History, April 1, 1998.
6   Keith Nibbelink, interview with Making History, March 19, 1998.
17 Harry Vermeer, interview by Making History, May 16, 1998.
18 Prepared remarks by George Wassenaar introducing Gary Vermeer at the presentation of the Pella Community Service Award, April 26, 1977.
19 Gary Vermeer, Customer Day speech.
20 Gary Vermeer, Antique Tractor Club speech.
21 Ibid.
22 Ibid.
23 Sources vary regarding the exact number of units manufactured. However, the product clearly proved to be an impetus that the fledgling company needed at that time.
24 Gary Vermeer, Customer Day speech.
25 Ibid.
26 Gary Vermeer, Customer Day speech.
27 Ibid.
28 Phil McCombs, "Making A Stand," Washington Post, July 30, 2001.

2 Growing a Company

1   Michael Soepers, in interview with Making History, May 4, 1998.
2   Information from public displays in Vermeer Museum.
3   Information from public displays in Vermeer Museum.
4   Harold Meinders, in a written tribute to Gary for his 80th birthday in 1998.
5   Vince Newendorp, in a written tribute to Gary for his 80th birthday in 1998.
6   In 2008, the board includes Gary Vermeer, Bob Vermeer, Mary Andringa, Mark De Cook, Robert Hardin, Lynn Horak, Derek Kaufman, and Mike Vermeer.
7   James Schaap, "Pella's Gary Vermeer," The Banner, April 26, 1982, p. 16.

3 Family Heritage

1   "The Vermeer Family History & Genealogy," the Vermeer family, Pella, Iowa, June 2006, pp 4-6.
2   Ibid., p. 7.
3   Ibid., p. 11.
4   Muriel Kool, "The History of Pella," <http://www.pellatuliptime.com/historical-village/history/pellahistory/history.html> , (August 1, 2007).
5   "John Brown and the Underground Railroad," Iowa History Project, <http://iagenweb.org/history/soi/soi37.htm> (August 1, 2007).
6   Dakota War of 1862, <http://en.wikipedia.org/wiki/Dakota_War_of_1862> (August 20, 2007).
7   Iowa History Project, "Stories of Iowa for Boys and Girls," 1931, <http://iagenweb.org/history/soi/soimp.htm>, August 1, 2007.
8   Vermeer history book, p. 12
9   Ibid.
10   Ibid.
11   History of Pella, Iowa, 1847-1987, volume 1, Curtis Media Corporation, Dallas, Texas, 1988, p. 640.
12   Ibid., p. 639.
13   Ibid., p. 640.
14   Ibid.
15   Ibid., p. 642.
16   Ibid.
17   John H. Vermeer during speech given at Gary and Matilda Vermeer's 50th wedding anniversary celebration, 1991.

18   Gary Vermeer, as interviewed on DVD titled "Senior Generation Speaks, 2006."
19   John H. Vermeer, as interviewed on "Senior Generation Speaks, 2006."
20   Gary Vermeer, "Senior Generation Speaks, 2006."
21   John H. Vermeer, during Vermeer's 50th wedding anniversary celebration.
22   Gary Vermeer, "Senior Generation Speaks, 2006."
23   History of Pella, p. 638.
24   History of Pella, p. 643.
25   History of Pella, p. 642.
26   Gary Vermeer during speech at his 50th wedding anniversary celebration, 1991.
27   Ibid.
28   Matilda Vermeer, interviewed by Stan Vermeer and Christy Vermeer, Colorado Springs, Colorado, July 2007.

4   Family Living

1   Agricultural Policy Analysis Center, "The Challenges of Peak Production: Drawing Lessons from the Past," April 6, 2007, <http://apacweb.ag.utk.edu/weekcol/348.html.> (July 14, 2007).
2   "The Iowa Wildlife Series," Iowa Association of Naturalists, <http://www.extension.iastate.edu/Publications/IAN601.pdf> (August 9, 2007).
3   Lean Manufacturing is a strategy to reduce lead time by eliminating waste in every area of production including customer relations, product design, supplier networks, and factory management. The goal is to produce what customers want, when they want it, at the highest quality while being productive and safe.
4   Matilda Vermeer, interviewed by Stan and Christy Vermeer, July 2007.
5   Ibid.
6   Stan Vermeer, during his interview of Matilda and Gary Vermeer, July 2007.
7   Matilda, interviewed by Stan and Christy.
8   Ibid.
9   Stan Vermeer, during his interview of Matilda and Gary.
10   Ibid.
11   Matilda, interviewed by Stan and Christy.
12   "How Many Americans Really Attend Church Each Week?" June 8, 2005, <http://theologica.blogspot.com/2005/06/how-many-americans-really-attend.html> July 14, 2007.
13   Stan Vermeer, interviewed by Making History, April 16, 1998.
14   Ibid.
15   Gary Vermeer, speech to Antique Tractor Club, March 21, 1997.

5   Always a Farmer

1   Dave Heinen, written tribute for Gary Vermeer's 80th birthday.

6   Gary, Hunter and Pilot

1   John H. Vermeer, written tribute to Gary for his 80th birthday, 1998.
2   Kevin Van Wyk, written tribute to Gary for his 80th birthday.
3   Among the others who hunted are Alfred Van Maaren, Clarence Spoelstra, Roger De
         Moss, Darrell De Nooy, Jerry Dowell, Bob Spencer, Jay Vermeer, Steve Vermeer, Ron
         Cowl, Lucas Emmert, Wes Van Maanen, Darren Van Maanen, Thomas Brand, Cameron
         Keske, Chris Laughlin, Jeffrey Braafhart, Dave Ver Steeg, Dan Vermeer, and Paul Smith.
4   Besides Gary, some of the other regulars in this group over the years included his brother,
         John H. Vermeer, as well as Roger Van Norden , Art Rus, Wayne Van Dyke, Rube and
         Kenny Steenhoek, Fred and Daryl De Nooy, Niles Van Dyke, Wade Van Dyke, Scott
         Renaud, Art Van Wolde, Arnold Van Zee, Rick Wester, Ken Zylstra, and Ward
         Van Dyke.
5   Piper PA-16 Clipper, Wikipedia,
         <http://en.wikipedia.org/wiki/Piper_PA-16_Clipper> (August 17, 2007).
6   The Beechcraft Bonanza, US Centennial of Flight Commision,
         <http://www.centennialofflight.gov/essay/GENERAL_AVIATION/bonanza/GA10.htm>
         (August 23, 2007).

7   Four Decades of Canada Fishing

1   Keith Nibbelink, a longtime employee, in his written 80th birthday tribute to Gary.
2   These comments by the Bob Taylor family, as well as the following four
         memories, are excerpted from tributes these people wrote in honor of Gary Vermeer's
         80th birthday.
3   Ontario, the Canadian Encyclopedia, <http://www.thecanadianencyclopedia.com/index.
         cfm?PgNm=TCE&Params=A1SEC891531> (June 1, 2007).
4   Ontario, The Canadian Encyclopedia, <http://www.thecanadianencyclopedia.com/
         index.cfm?PgNm=TCE&Params=A1ARTA0005936> (June 1, 2007).
5   Ken and Lois Schepel, birthday tribute.
6   Ken Weller, birthday tribute.
7   Dale Van Donselaar, birthday tribute.

In Search of a Better Way
The Lives and Legacies of Gary and Matilda Vermeer
299

8   Howard and Lola Vander Hart, birthday tribute.

9   Allan Beyer, birthday tribute.

10   Rev. Henry Vermeer, birthday tribute.

11   Jerry Lundy, birthday tribute.

8   An Adventurous Spirit

1   A skit by Allison and David, at Gary and Matilda's 50th wedding anniversary celebration.

2   Information from script of Gary and Matilda's 50th anniversary celebration.

3   Sacred Sites, Martin Gray, <www.sacredsites.com/asia/cambodia/angkor_wat.html>, (June 1, 2007).

4   American Park Network, <www.americanparknetwork.com/parkinfo/gc/walking/trails.html>, (June 26, 2007).

5   Tanzania Tourist Board, <http://tanzaniatouristboard.com/places_to_go/national_parks_reserves/ngorongoro>, (June 6, 2007).

6   Scrapbook compiled by Christy Vermeer about the trip.

7   Australian Antarctica Division—Antarctic Convergence, <www.aad.gov.au/default.asp?casid=6558>, (June 16, 2007).

8   Christy's scrapbook.

9   Penguins Around the World, <www.siec.k12.in.us/~west/proj/penguins/gentoo.html> (June 25, 2007).

10   Christy's scrapbook.

11   Ibid.

12   Ibid.

13   Ibid.

14   Wikipedia, <http:/en.wikipedia.org/wiki/North_Pole>, (June 16, 2007).

9   Giving to the Community

1   Gary and Matilda believe in the Biblical concept of tithing, generally described as the practice of giving ten percent of income back to God. Gary borrowed an amount equal to about ten percent of the company's profit to give away—an amount quite likely derived from his belief in tithing. A more in-depth discussion of the couple's belief in this concept is contained in Chapter 10.

2   Making History research notes.

3   Making History research notes.

4   The Bible, II Corinthians 9:11.

5   "Top 50 Iowa Foundations by Total Giving, circa 2005," The Foundation Center, <http://foundationcenter.org/findfunders/statistics/pdf/10_top50_tg/2005/ia_05.pdf> (October 5, 2007).

6   Making History research notes.

7   "Vermeer Charitable Gifts $350,000 to Dordt," Dordt College news release, May 17, 2007, <http://www.dordt.edu/cgi-bin/news/get_news.pl?id=2403> (September 12, 2007).

8   This list, obtained from the hospital's archival records, includes the members of the original steering committee as of January 18, 1958. Within a couple weeks, the committee was expanded and quite a few others became involved.

9   Pella Hospital's archival records.

10   Making History research notes.

11   "Hospital Drive Goes Over the Top," *Pella Chronicle*, June 26, 1958, p. 1.

12   "Hospital addition drive goes over $3 million goal," *Pella Chronicle*, date unknown.

13   City of Pella website, <http://cityofpella.com/aquatics.htm> (9/12/2007).

14   Matilda needn't have worried. The Dutch Buffet stayed open for 20 years.

15   Most information about Gary's involvement with the theatre comes from the autobiography of Martin Heerema, who was Central's vice president of financial affairs in 1960 when the idea first surfaced.

10   Values of a Lifetime

1   "What A Day That Will Be," words and music by Jim Hill, <http://www.my.homewithgod.com/heavenlymidis2/whataday.html> (Sept. 22, 2007).

2   Rehoboth Christian Schools, <http://www.rcsnm.org/aboutUs/index.php> (Sept. 25, 2007).

3   Vermeer History Book, p. 7.

4   Hearts is a card game, and the governing body of the Christian Reformed Church (Synod) had warned members against card playing in 1928.

5   A concept established in the Old Testament of the Bible, tithing generally refers to a Christian's practice of giving ten percent of what he or she earns back to God. It has been an important principle to Gary and Matilda. Quite likely, a belief in tithing is what first prodded Gary and his cousin Ralph to give money away to charity after the company became profitable. And a belief in tithing continues today to be the backbone of the Vermeer Charitable Foundation's practice of giving.

6   Gary and Matilda, interview by Stan Vermeer and Christy Vermeer, Colorado Springs, Colorado, July 2007.

7   Gary Vermeer speech, 50th wedding anniversary celebration.
8   Interview by Stan and Christy, July 2007.
9   The home was originally built with four bedrooms, but the Vermeers converted one of
         the original four bedrooms into a larger bathroom in 2007 to accommodate
         Gary's mobility needs.

*All quotations are from interviews conducted by The Write Place in 2007 and 2008, unless
footnoted otherwise.*

In Search of a Better Way
The Lives and Legacies of Gary and Matilda Vermeer
303

Acknowledgements

The following acknowledgements are a collaborative effort between the Vermeer family and those who created *In Search of a Better Way*.

Thank you to Gary and Matilda Vermeer for sharing the story of their lives, and for the people who have walked beside them along the way. Thank you to Stan and Alma Vermeer, Bob and Lois Vermeer, and Mary and Dale Andringa for all of their support, and for continuing the legacy with their own lives, and through their children and grandchildren. Thanks to family, friends, coworkers, and peers who so generously shared their memories. Your words have enriched this story.

Thank you to the people of Vermeer for the hard work and commitment that has seen the company through 60 successful years in business. Because of you—the employees, dealers, and supporters who create the larger Vermeer Family—this story is fuller and more far-reaching than Gary and Matilda could have ever imagined.

To the host of people who made this publication possible and worked diligently to share these words with accuracy and all the color it deserves, thank you.

Thank you to author Carol Van Klompenburg, founder and owner of The Write Place in Pella, a writing and graphic arts service since 1995. She has written several books and plays and has taught nonfiction writing at two Iowa colleges. Carol has an MA in Theatre Arts from the University of Minnesota and a BA in English from Dordt College.

Thank you to author Donna Biddle, a graduate of the University of Missouri School of Journalism. Donna covered local and state government and politics for more than 10 years as a reporter for newspapers in Missouri and Nebraska. She also worked in corporate communications, and joined The Write Place as a writer in 1999. She continues to work for the Pella-based business from her home in Kearney, Nebraska, where she lives with her husband and two children.

Thank you to Tilly Woodward for the original artwork used in the cover design, and the portrait of Gary and Matilda. Tilly is Curator of Academic and Community Outreach at Grinnell College's Faulconer Gallery. Her work has been exhibited in more than 192 museums and galleries nationally and can be found in museum, corporate, and private collections throughout the country. Tilly graduated from Phillips Academy, Andover, in Andover, Massachusetts, and holds a BFA from the Kansas City Art Institute, and an MFA from the University of Kansas.

Thank you to Teri Vos for her detailed review and attention to this project, from organizing and editing to coordinating and critiquing. Teri is a graduate of Dordt College and has worked extensively in the publications, communications, and public relations fields. She currently focuses on those areas for Vermeer Corporation, and lives near Pella with her husband and three children.

Thank you to those with The Write Place and Vermeer for all your help. Special thanks to Alexis Thomas for design work, Kathleen Evenhouse for overseeing photographs, and to Christy Vermeer and the Vermeer archives and museum staff for providing many of the photos.

Finally, for the past, present, and future, all praise to the Creator.

Thanks be to God!